I0333427

Gustaf Sobin

Collected Poems

Shearsman Library Vol. 23

Other Books by Gustaf Sobin

Poetry

Wind Chrysalid's Rattle (Montemora, New York, 1980;
2nd ed. Shearsman Books, Bristol, 2023)
Celebration of the Sound Through (Montemora, New York, 1982)
The Earth as Air (New Directions, New York, 1984)
Sicilian Miniatures (Cadmus Editions, San Francisco, 1986)
Voyaging Portraits (New Directions, New York, 1988)
Breaths' Burials (New Directions, New York, 1995)
By the Bias of Sound: Selected Poems 1974–1994 (Talisman House, Jersey City, 1995)
Towards the Blanched Alphabets (Talisman House, Jersey City, 1998)
Articles of Light & Elation (Cadmus Editions, San Francisco, 1998)
In the Name of the Neither (Talisman House, Jersey City, 2002)
The Places as Preludes (Talisman House, Jersey City, 2005)
Uncollected Poems (Shearsman Books, Bristol, 2025)

Fiction

Venus Blue (Bloomsbury, London, 1991; Little, Brown, New York, 1992;
2nd ed., Shearsman Books, Bristol, 2025)
Dark Mirrors (Bloomsbury, London, 1992; 2nd ed., Shearsman Books, Bristol, 2025)
The Fly-Truffler (Bloomsbury, London, 1999; Norton, New York, 2000)
In Pursuit of a Vanishing Star (Norton, New York, 2002)

Essays

Luminous Debris: Reflecting on Vestige in Provence and Languedoc (University of California Press, Berkeley, 1999)
Ladder of Shadows: Reflecting on Medieval Vestige in Provence and Languedoc (University of California Press, Berkeley, 2009)
Aura: Last Essays (Counterpath, Denver, 2009)

Translations

Ideograms in China by Henri Michaux (New Directions, New York, 2002)
The Brittle Age and Returning Upland by René Char (Counterpath, Denver, 2009)

For Children

The Tale of the Yellow Triangle (George Braziller, New York, 1973)

Gustaf Sobin

Collected Poems

Edited by Esther Sobin,
Andrew Joron and Andrew Zawacki

Introduction by Andrew Joron & Andrew Zawacki

Shearsman Books

SECOND EDITION
Published in the United Kingdom in 2025 by
Shearsman Books, PO Box 4239, Swindon SN3 9FN

www.shearsman.com

Shearsman Books Ltd Registered Office: 30–31 St. James Place, Mangotsfield, Bristol BS16 9JB
(this address not for correspondence)

EU AUTHORISED REPRESENTATIVE:
Lightning Source France, 1 Av. Johannes Gutenberg, 78310 Maurepas, France
Email: compliance@lightningsource.fr

ISBN 978-1-84861-994-4
[Also available in hardcover, ISBN 978-1-84861-998-2]

ACKNOWLEDGEMENTS
The first edition of this book was published in 2010 by Talisman House Publishers, Greenfield, MA, U.S.A. The individual volumes collected here were first published in the U.S.A. by Montemora, New Directions, and Talisman House Publishers.

We are grateful to New Directions Publishing Corp, New York, for permission to reprint three volumes within these covers:

BREATHS' BURIALS, copyright ©1992, 1993, 1993, 1994, 1995 by Gustaf Sobin. Reprinted by permission of New Directions Publishing Corp.

VOYAGING PORTRAITS, copyright ©1984, 1985, 1986, 1987, 1988 by Gustaf Sobin. Reprinted by permission of New Directions Publishing Corp.

THE EARTH AS AIR, copyright ©1982, 1983, 1984 by Gustaf Sobin. Reprinted by permission of New Directions Publishing Corp.

Works included in the *New Poems* section were first published in *26, Denver Quarterly, Hambone*, and *Talisman.*

CONTENTS

Celebration of the Sound Through

I. Wave's Scaffolds

II. Nenuphar

The Earth as Air

I. At the Flaked Edges

II. Carnets

III. The Wizened Shrine

IV. The Earth as Air: An Ars Poetica

Voyaging Portraits

1. Of Neither Wind Nor Anemones

II. Against a Bleached Viridian

III. A Portrait of the Self as Instrument of Its Syllables

IV. Along America's Edges

V. Of the Four-Winged Cherubim as Signature

Breaths' Burials

I. On the Fragility of Idols

II. Lines from Pietro Longhi

III. The Densities of Naught

IV. Odes of Estrangement

Towards the Blanched Alphabets

I. Under the Bright Orchards

II. Late Bronze, Early Iron: A Journey Book

III. Substantia Separata

IV. Reading Sarcophagi: An Essay

V. Like the Opening and Closing of Clouds

In the Name of the Neither

The Places as Preludes

New Poems

VERTICAL TRACKING

Introduction by Andrew Joron and Andrew Zawacki

Gustaf Sobin lived in the south of France for over forty years. He had discovered, in 1962, in his mid-twenties, the poetry of René Char, via a Random House translation edited by Jackson Matthews, with a blurb from William Carlos Williams. His encounter with Char's work spurred the aspiring poet to abandon his native United States, a place associated in his mind with crass commercialism and a Cold War freeze on aesthetic innovation, for the vineyards, cypresses, and olive groves of the Luberon, a mountainous region he believed to be the locus of primal purity and poetic flourishing.

Through the intercession of a mutual friend, the young Bostonian was able to meet Char in Paris. As Sobin later recalled, "Char, an immensely warm man of unpredictable humor, urged me to visit Provence. If I admired his poetry so much, he said, I should, at least, see where the poems themselves came from."[1] Sobin returned briefly to the States to sell his belongings and arrived in Provence in February 1963. With financial assistance from Char, he purchased an abandoned silk cocoonery in Goult, a medieval village in the Vaucluse, not far from where his exemplar lived. Sobin converted the old building into a residence and added, a short walk away, a *cabanon* containing a modest writing desk and chair, a manual typewriter, a shelf for a few books and dry lavender, two windows, a cot.

This simple hut, with its main window opening onto the wide fields of Provence, would serve as Sobin's singular workspace from the beginning of his apprenticeship to Char until the end of his days. Here, in this writing cabin, over the course of four decades, Sobin produced eight books of poetry, four novels, three volumes of essays, and two books of translation. Gustaf Sobin died in Provence, a few months before his seventieth birthday, in summer 2005.

Having lived abroad may, in part, account for why Sobin has often been seen – or unseen – as a somewhat minor, mandarin poet, claiming a venerated group of admirers and apologists but lacking the wider public that many writers, uneasy descendants of Kafka's hunger artist, often welcome

[1] Ed Foster, 'An Interview with Gustaf Sobin,' *Talisman: A Journal of Contemporary Poetry and Poetics* 10 (Spring 1993): 38. The number contains a feature on Sobin's work.

even as they abjure its intrusion. Sobin's writing, unusually attentive to the natural world, language's spoors and spirals, and the mysteries that ligature one to the other, is a subtle form of communication that has refused to beg for attention, demanding instead the patient, voluntary hospitality of the reader. This is an exigency not easily heard, let alone answered, by participants in an increasingly careerist American literary milieu, where prizes and pedigrees, university prestige, and divisive politico-aesthetic loyalties have come to dominate the would-be poetic discourse.

On the contrary, as Theodore Enslin once lauded, Sobin was an amateur, in the highest sense of the word: a lover of the thing itself. Sobin's was a lifelong investigation of, investment in, and vigilance toward the tiniest, most peripheral of objects and abstractions; he sought to glorify them like Hopkins, whom he claimed as his favorite poet, and offered antiphons to "the psalm, burnt / to a glass / whisper," that Traherne had penned with a similarly quiet profile. "My entire work," Sobin once confided, "might be seen as a transcript of sorts, celebrating margins."[2]

§

Sobin's approach to poetry places him not only at the margins of the American literary scene but, even more resolutely, at the margins of language itself. Meaning, for Sobin, is something perpetually blown, scattered, scuttled, gutted, obliterated – yet, at the same time, something incendiary, reverberant, resonant, shimmering. Situated at the very edge of the sayable, Sobin's poems offer transcriptions of the *isn't* – a recurrent word, in his usage, suspended between verb and noun, and caught in the act of contracting against its own negation. More than any other contemporary poet, Sobin possessed a Heraclitean awareness of negation as a form of (re) generation: his insistent return to the instant of the isn't represents not the stopping, but the starting point of poetic motion. Sobin's line becomes a "traced erasure,"[3] alive to the vaporous echoes of the null, the naught, the neither.

Moreover, the propensity of language to negate being, to stand in place of the thing signified, in the manner of a mirror or a veil (further Sobin

---

[2] Tedi López Mills, 'Epilogo, Entrevista con Gustaf Sobin,' in *Matrices de viento y de sombra: Antología Poética 1980–1998*, edited and translated by Tedi López Mills (Mexico City: Hotel Ambos Mundos, 1999) 176. English text printed in Gustaf Sobin, *Uncollected Poems* (Bristol: Shearsman Books, 2025).

[3] 'Late Bronze, Early Iron: A Journey Book,' in the present volume.

keywords), is frequently registered in Sobin's work as a play of reflexivity, a flexing of meaning against its own iteration (in the later poems especially, this endlessly reflected vanishing point is identified as 'you', an address to the self as other). Here, the word – as a stand-in for something other than itself – is finally understood to be an index of exile, a vestige or relic of original being: "for language, as you'd learnt, was never more than the arbitrary imprint of a violated silence."[4] Sobin's self-exile from his native land thus finds an echo in his poetic practice.

Yet, in life and in language, Sobin was at home in exile. Far from feeling alienated from a Kulchur inimical to any notion of reception, "It's almost an advantage," he avowed, "living at a distance in which one's own language is used – almost exclusively – for writing. The words take on a kind of buoyancy, a kind of freshness. They're free of so much exhausted usage" and "day-to-day attrition."[5] The poet perceived his adopted home of Provence, with its deep, historical layers of human occupation from the Neolithic onward, as a speaking landscape, as living vestige. The Provençal earth, with its breath of the past, was translated readily into the breath of the poem – the earth as air, indeed. Here, it was possible to go "delving, as you did, for echo," finding the "impression, everywhere, of aftermath: of having entered, already, an after-world; of muttering to yourself in some kind of after-language." Not with the intention of preserving the past but rather, by a poetic act, of turning time inside out: "would, if you could, precede vestige. / reach, that is, far enough back that you might begin, finally, projecting forwards."[6]

Sobin's poetic project is revealed, then, as "the resuscitation of so many suppressed ur-words by the bias of a yet-to-be articulated grammar."[7] These ur-words, the original Saying, have yet to be spoken.

§

In 'A Portrait of the Self as Instrument of Its Syllables,' Sobin describes the formation of his own poetic identity as an encounter, not only with the primal landscape of Provence, where he "read / rocks. Read // walls," but also with the *ur*-texts of the poets he regarded as his teachers. Claiming Blake and Char as "my // first masters," Sobin named myriad

[4] 'Transparent Itineraries: 1994,' in the present volume.
[5] Foster, 'An Interview with Gustaf Sobin' 36.
[6] 'Late Bronze, Early Iron: A Journey Book,' in the present volume.
[7] 'Transparent Itineraries: 1999,' in the present volume.

other influences, spanning from Wordsworth and the impossibly high Romantic aspirations for poetry and 'the poet' to the more recent example of American contemporaries like Michael McClure; "from // Mallarmé" he derived "that / rush // of crushed / shadow, and Shakespeare, that / pearl, its / black // sphericity…" In this poem, Sobin also cites Hölderlin – but largely in relation to Heidegger, whom Sobin met "for several summers running," when the German philosopher would come to visit Char. Along with Sobin, the sole American present for the occasion, a small number of French poets and philosophers would gather "in the deep shade of René Char's plane tree" and listen to Heidegger and his host discuss "a single, lapidary fragment of Heraclitus, say, or Empedocles" for hours. "One could only feel privileged," Sobin later recalled, "to witness their exchange: two giants discussing a handful of words from the dawn of civilization."[8]

Many of the issues raised by Heidegger's philosophy would become integral to Sobin's poetics: the relation between Being and beings; the insistence on language as ontologically central; the fraught quest for authenticity in the face of fear, anxiety, death, and the faceless "they"; the fourfold gathering of earth, sky, mortals, and gods; wariness about the encroaching dangers of unchecked technology; worry regarding historical amnesia and the forgetting of that forgetfulness; the phenomenological play of appearance and concealment; the doctrine of care; and the fundamental human need to build and to dwell. At the same time, however, Sobin's work is partial to the Lévinasian rejoinder to Heidegger. The Jewish thinker had accused Heidegger's ontology of a pernicious egoism, a spatial and temporal privileging of the self over its surround, including the human community, and sought to devise an ethics that would instead place the other always already before 'me,' relegating the 'I' to a posture of respect, of infinite responsibility, even guilt.

Sobin's poems, relentlessly pitched toward someone else, whether *in situ* or *in absentia*, privilege possible accords between the first person and a second. His insistence on the poem as a passage, of the poetry volume as volute, seems to have been inflected by the interpersonal repositioning endemic to the philosophical turn toward alterity. For an author, *chez* Sobin, exists only to usher the poem forward, at which point he disappears, while poem itself is likewise only a vanishing point to a more absolute end: each is "nothing, in itself," he writes in *The Earth as Air*, "an otherwise-isn't, except for the syllables, either side, that channel, sluice, project it forth."[9]

---

[8] Foster, 'An Interview with Gustaf Sobin' 36.

[9] 'The Earth as Air: An Ars Poetica,' in the present volume.

That the poet is finally exempted from the poem hints at a latter-day, secular mysticism, a negative theology recoded for aesthetics. Constantly juxtaposing eternity and the ephemeral, Sobin's work traffics in paradigms of divinity, while eschewing the presence of any orthodox god. Haunted by an evacuated totality, some deity in default, his poems are imbued with what, speaking of the late painter Ambrogio Magnaghi, he called a "lingering religiosity."[10] This imperative to develop a religious surrogate is hardly specific to Sobin, who warranted his tendencies with examples from antiquity. "Since at least the outset of the Neolithic, ten thousand years earlier," Sobin said in a late interview, "human societies have addressed – in supplication – invisible auditoria. Have basked in the radiance of some form of immanent response."[11] He considered this hopeful, albeit withheld reply as the nonetheless "indispensable complement to an all-too-precarious existence on earth." While the divine cosmology and its assurances have "undergone eclipse," thereby having "deprived us of our most privileged form of address," Sobin was adamant in asserting that

> What hasn't vanished, however, is the need – call it the psychic imperative – that such an address exist. Long after the addressee has vanished, after the omniscient mirror has dissolved and its transcendent dimension been dismantled, demystified, deconstructed, there remains – I insist – that psychic imperative deeply inscribed within the innermost regions of our being. We can't do, it would seem, without something that isn't... Only in the poem, I find, in so many stray bars of speculative music, can that trajectory still be traced.

Whether Sobin's brand of 'religion without religion' hails from a quitted Christianity, as with Heidegger, or from the fraught Judaic heritage implied by Paul Celan's tragic invocations to "you," Sobin declared no affiliation with any established denomination. Indebted to Saint Augustine and to the Zohar, to Meister Eckhart and Martin Buber alike, Sobin's writing honors devotion wherever it is practiced.

§

The most obvious and eccentric formal tendency in Sobin's verse is what he termed its "vertical tracking," or its impetus to spill, in thrall to gravity's

[10] 'The Miracle Depicted,' *Ambrogio Magnaghi* (Milan: Skira, 2004) 11.
[11] Leonard Schwartz, 'Interview with Gustaf Sobin,' *Verse* 20.2&3 (2004): 110.

pull. This laddering of the lyric was "influenced by film," he once conceded, where "cadence is determined by an inexorable movement downward," one frame replacing another. More usually, though, Sobin's impulse to erect his poems earth- and skyward hailed from a commitment to the physical world and its organic processes: "don't write a poem: grow it," he remarked, "the poem grows out of the poem, not out of one's own, particular intellect."[12] Sobin saw his compositional method as "natural" and "innate," like training a vine, rather than "intellectually acquired," and trusted that breaking with linear prosody meant a divorce from positivist thought.[13] Indeed, phrases in Sobin's semantics commonly begin without capital letters, which he argued would "set up a tiny, typographical hierarchy" that was "slightly imperious,"[14] and many lines lack a subject altogether, beginning instead with a verb, to indicate how the universe verses itself.

In his 'A Few Stray Comments on the Cultivation of the Lyric,' Sobin insisted that "the poem is verbal, rather than nounal," that it should render nouns "light and evocative," should "verbalize" them.[15] Like Emerson, he vaunted transition over stasis, in pursuit of a "discourse of continuous becoming," but his poems do not neglect tangible stuff or reject words that, in their tactility, slow or stagger a poem's linguistic rush.[16] Sobin valorized Oppen's "focused intensity" toward "investing the particular with its all-too-lost significance,"[17] and in Black Mountain and Objectivism he learned to be "scrupulously mindful of particulars, discreet if not downright self-effacing in regard to the personal self, and charged with an innate faith in the power of language as a vehicle of revaluations."[18] There is as much 'against' in Sobin's work as 'toward,' as much bunching, clotting, and interruption, à la Celan's constricted nominal constructions, as 'unto.' This oscillating, "catch- / flow" duality colludes with his recurrent tropes of respiration, mirroring, lovemaking, potential and kinetic energies.

Some of Sobin's formal proclivities, as he happily admitted, were less "innate" than learned. He credited Creeley, for example, with instructing him in how to breathe, to turn or enjamb a line, rig the poem as a "vertical

---

[12] Gustaf Sobin, 'A Few Stray Comments on the Cultivation of the Lyric,' *Talisman* 10 (Spring 1993): 41.

[13] Foster, 'An Interview with Gustaf Sobin' 31.

[14] López Mills, 'Epilogo, Entrevista con Gustaf Sobin' 178.

[15] Sobin, 'A Few Stray Comments on the Cultivation of the Lyric' 43.

[16] Foster, 'An Interview with Gustaf Sobin' 34.

[17] Foster, 'An Interview with Gustaf Sobin' 29.

[18] López Mills, 'Epilogo, Entrevista con Gustaf Sobin' 181–182.

gesture" cascading and terracing downward, rather than spanning across.[19] But Sobin honed this formal gauntness to a radical degree, webbing the page to where individual morphemes snap like a brittle branch in winter, or else bloom as a flower unfolds in spring. Linguistic anthropologists such as Benjamin Lee Whorf and Edward Sapir had showed Sobin, in his own staccato music, "how the / least / shift in syntax, tense- / perception, would / re- // set the / heavens."[20] His ambition and humility alike were aligned to such a recalibration. This generative process is frequently figured sensually, often erotically, as the poems lavish among intertwined bodies, seeds, germination, liquid and spasms, blowing and swallowing.

Yet alongside incarnated desire and celebrated corporeality, Sobin is never far from asceticism, either, the relinquishment of identity, a reduction to what is "blanched" and unpretentious — the minimal necessity. Language as effulgence, caesura as severest praise: these are the extremes between which Sobin's poems wander, now in obsessive concentration, now rapt to the parenthetical. The vocal thrust is up- and outward, as exhalation rising, air returning to air, even as the written tumbles, bound for the ground, as an excavation, a mode of depth and of density. A centripetal graffiti, then, married to centrifugal song.

To the extent that Sobin conceived writing as obeying "an inherent tendency within language to unspell, unspeak, divest itself of its own nomenclature in an attempt to touch upon the untouchable, utter the unutterable,"[21] his 'Transparent Itineraries' prove an intriguing exception. Cutting through and across individual books, stitching the volumes together even as they fray the very notion of a discrete book, the 'Transparent Itineraries,' which Sobin began in 1979, are a mostly contiguous string (there are none for the second half of the 1980s) of annual poetic sequences that seek not, as in his other lyrics, to move organically "from a place, a locus, a set of material circumstances, to a proposition," but rather to assemble the season's leftovers.[22] Oriented horizontally, less fractured or intuitive than his lyrics, the series is conceptually informed by Duncan's 'Passages' and 'The Structure of Rime,' except that Sobin engaged in a conservationist mosaic, recycling the year's compost, collaging a poem as an archive of remaindered matter.

---

[19] Foster, 'An Interview with Gustaf Sobin' 31.
[20] 'A Portrait of the Self as Instrument of Its Syllables,' in the present volume.
[21] Schwartz, 'Interview with Gustaf Sobin,' 112.
[22] Foster, 'An Interview with Gustaf Sobin' 26.

If Duncan had bequeathed Sobin a notion of language as Orphic, ontological source, of poetry as an act of "air, that / ayre exultant,"[23] the 'Transparent Itineraries' claimed their start in Sobin's own, otherwise failed fits and starts. "Essentially ephemeral in nature," he said of the series, "each passage lasts exactly the length of its implication: its 'sign'... One elicits another, each linking – transparently – with the next, as the poem moves across the broken landscapes of the experiential."

Marking yet another procedural departure, Sobin's later poems increasingly partake of extended intellectual, if not academic, exploration. 'Reading Sarcophagi: An Essay,' as the latter part of its title announces, traces half a millennium of history to Constantine's conversion, spanning eleven pages and featuring endnotes, signaled by number within the text. Similarly, the even longer 'Late Bronze, Early Iron: A Journey Book' examines the emergence, between 700 and 550 B.C., of the mercantile exchange system. Reaching less for the ineffable than for an irretrievable history, many poems, from *Towards the Blanched Alphabets* onward, eschew a seminal object of meditative contemplation characteristic of Sobin's earliest, haiku-like lyrics, and instead pursue, with increasing abstraction and logic, the decline of entire societies.

These poems, along with others like 'Barocco: An Essay' and 'On Imminence: An Essay,' were written more or less concurrently with a research project on Gallo-Roman antiquity that would eventuate as *Luminous Debris: Reflecting on Vestige in Provence and Languedoc*, one of Sobin's best-loved books. Ostensibly a collection of anthropological essays, the constituent meditations are as 'poetic' as some of the later poems are rigorously 'essayistic,' and while written in prose they are nonetheless, like the lyrics, devoted to what Sobin termed a "vertical reading" of southern France.

§

The present volume collects all the poems that Sobin published during his lifetime, in eight full-length books, as well as those residual lyrics (placed in an order agreed upon by his daughter Esther Sobin, Talisman House publisher Ed Foster, and us) that constitute about half an untitled, final manuscript. A late bloomer, Sobin completed his first book, *Wind Chrysalid's Rattle*, at the age of forty, and it would not appear until five years later, from the Montemora Foundation, as a supplement to their magazine

[23] 'A Portrait of the Self as Instrument of Its Syllables,' in the present volume.

of international poetry and poetics. Montemora would publish his second book, *Celebration of the Sound Through*, as well.

Meanwhile, art critic, novelist, and fellow expatriate John Berger had introduced Sobin's work to Charles Tomlinson who, in turn, recommended it to James Laughlin. The founder and editor of New Directions ran Sobin's poems in numerous numbers of the annual *New Directions Anthology in Prose and Poetry*, eventually publishing his next trio of books. After Laughlin's death, Sobin was released from the New Directions list, publishing the four books comprising his later career, including a selected poems, with Talisman House.

For better or worse, this *Collected Poems* does not take into account a dozen or so chapbooks and pamphlets, most of them limited editions, occasionally letter-pressed, that, from the mid-1960s, had been printed in the U.S.A., England, and France by Arcturus, Cadmus, Grenfell, Oasis, PAB, and Shearsman. Many of those editions were subsequently collected in the larger compilations that feature in this volume, while others – seen by the author as being outside the main trajectory of his work – have been brought together in the *Uncollected Poems*, published by Shearsman Books in 2025, along with poems from journals which the author did not later include in any formal collection. For this *Collected*, we opted, deferentially, to reproduce all the work Sobin considered worthy of book publication, whatever authority his judgment might convey.

His literary papers are now housed in the Beinecke archive at Yale – an appropriateness that Sobin, who meticulously catalogued extant drafts and correspondence shortly before his death, would appreciate. Half a century earlier, as a Brown University undergraduate, he had worked his way through the Eliot and Pound holdings, among many others, in the Gertrude Stein collection in nearby New Haven. So in some ways his poetry has returned to its archival origin.

Needless to say, this volume does not include Sobin's quartet of novels, published over a decade, the most successful of which, by far, was *The Fly Truffler*. First published in England in 1999 and in the U.S. the following year, that novel appeared in translated editions in Germany, The Netherlands, Portugal, France, and Taiwan. "If poetry could be called the realm of the unexpected," Sobin once ventured, then prose "is that of the plan, the foreseen."[24] His fictions might be considered the level, deliberately constructed counterpoints to his more natural, vertical lyrics. Sobin's further experiments with narrative, scarce or at best oblique in the poems,

[24] Foster, 'An Interview with Gustaf Sobin' 34.

manifested themselves in a series of short stories and a co-authored children's book.

His translations of Henri Michaux are available from New Directions in a boxed, signed, limited edition, while his renderings of René Char into English were published in 2009 by Counterpath Press, as *The Brittle Age and Returning Upland.* The second volume in Sobin's planned triptych of anthropological essays, *Ladder of Shadows: Reflecting on Medieval Vestige in Provence and Languedoc* has been published by the University of California Press, and Counterpath Press issued the third, never finished book, under the title *Aura: Last Essays.*

§

Sobin liked to think of his own itinerary, in poetry and in the poetry, as having begun with "becoming," progressed through "being," and having concluded, precisely without conclusion, in "non-being." That seems an appropriate trajectory for a poet so deeply concerned with the modalities of existence and extinction. We are, he worried, at the end of history, but only that it may yet begin once again, renovated by none other than the poet. Who, in a final act of self-sacrifice, would not live to witness the transformation that his words, of their own will-to-powerlessness, would work. The poet, touched by the "null," the "no-breath" that the poem carries "within," himself would become nothing more – and nothing less – than a noble passage; he would pass. While "poetry," Sobin said one afternoon near Avignon, "cannot but survive."

Wind Chrysalid's Rattle

I

Wind Chrysalid's Rattle

(1973)

... c'est que tout a été donné aux hommes, dès l'origine, mais sous une forme mobile: ils transportent avec eux, tout au long de leur migration, la totalité de ce qui doit être créé.

—Lucien Sebag

DOMINION

not light.
not even   the seeds of   light.   but its   black humus,
its dampness   dreaming through the flesh,

the breath   still numb,   its   shimmering globe   still
wordless, imminent: an opal
of   trolling falcons!

SIGNS

what matters   is what the shadow   says;
is reading the cloud, and the   spastic drift
of dragonflies
over the glass-headed meadow.

is earth, its ciphers.   its membrane   of sounds.
is one's life   risked, a miracle
within a lizard's eyes!

ISN'T THAT'S ALMOST

isn't
that's almost (its vastness, infinitesimal: a glint
in the voice's wondrous shadows). *isn't*

that dreams itself: the translucent herd of its
kisses driven, ineluctable, the

earth germinal driven into the absence that *is.*

THAT THE UNIVERSE IS CHRYSALID

(Blake's Birthday)

That the universe is chrysalid.

That all things that are, are continuous emanations.

That their being is a perpetual becoming.

That becoming is the breath of lust. And that lust is perfection.

That all increments are equal.

The spore is the clavicord of the tree.

The clavicord is lust.

That in creating we extend the very energy that creates us.

That this extension is space.

That space, the space we move through, and dwell in, is made up of the
infinitesimal crystals that we murmur.

Music hears.

That creation is momentum made perceptible.

The attempt to store or isolate momentum is tyranny.

Not sequence, but elaboration.

That genesis is a wind.

The rock ripples; the night swims.

That the eyes are forever swifter than their green mirrors.

That structure is shadow.

That music should catch fire and flame into gesture, motion, deed.

That the past hasn't yet happened.

That only the edge is dominion.

Only the edge secretes.

That our lust is lightness. Acceleration.

And what we call the 'stillness' is the inconceivable velocity of our flesh, thinking in the same space-cadence as the universe.

The thrust of a single whisper.

The lymph, the lightning!

That life, in its ecstatic throes, touches the resplendence of death.

That the senses shall iridesce into their infinite sensations.

That we become, ultimately, the space we've created.

Blossoming generatrix, and genius of our every breath.

HELIX

Liquid, the dawn's
green axe.

The sheer agility of wrists,
calves,
of the eyes swimming
into the earth's
first clouds.

Why wait?
What holds?
The breath sprouts,
sprouts flutes,
the horn's spiralling glass.

Villages rise
in wheels of rich dust,
while a creature
begs for herself,
buoyed
in the glittering arms of her voice.

THE TURBAN

what is   writes itself.   the mauve-gold   claws
          of the honeysuckle
                    make   perfect cantatas.
what isn't   except in its   black incipience
   is breath: breath   reaching
   into the thick globe
          of its whispers (its seed   wrought
with the wisdom of   an ultimate resonance);
   is muscle   flowering into muscle;
   is   hair, shuddering like a   liquid
into its vacuum of   light;
   is light, itself,   flooding the stars. . . . .

   earth, asleep, in   the music of its spores,
   earth, asleep, in   the music of its spores,
      the body is   blown through the tongue

into a perfect turban of bees   and deep thunder.

HYMN: FOR THE SERPENT

the hardest: *seeing* the *black quartz*   burn
        in each creature   each thing,
                        the saint's task,   living
its illumination, and never making it   one's own,
appropriating,   or expelling it into   myth:
  another's.   but to gut the   shadows

in the deep canyon. to release the   serpent,

seeing   not the scales in   their quick glitter,
but the *flame*:   the black   immaculate light
  it's made of, and moves in, and *is.*   *creation*

  winding   chemically   through its creature.

~

separate   not caged in   the senses
      the cold prejudice of   sight (the universe
twisted   to the perspective of   self)

  but the chord, echoing   in the clear flesh,
    the *flame*,   its resonance, incarnate,
            ringing in each,   separate,

nobody's light but   the splendor's   in each
that each *sees* (*echoing*,   naked) in   the other.

~

the saint
throning in the same *flames*   as the serpent
            (his mind, blinded   in light,
             the bones of his mirror, blinded) *sees*
through the   serpent's form
the black   ecstatic *coil,*
the *quartz,*   the blossoming *quartz* in   both of them
   climb, *quintessential*
   (as the creature   blinks in the wind
         unaware, and rides
         toward its   rock)
he *sees* it:
its miracle live: *murderous,*   *innocent,*   *equal.*

HELIX

Out of our red icons
we reach,
our wounds
studded with eyes,
whispers,
claws;
with slow flares
of tentacles
thirsting the earth
we exude,
the glittering lust
we stutter.

Spectral
will we alight,
and rooting
hollow a seed?

Strange hands,
spent voices,
the breath, ever migrant.
Flight
through the charred language,
the wind's
flaked walls
hide
the immediate.

NOTES ON SOUND, SPEECH, SPEECH-CRYSTALS AND THE CELESTIAL ECHO

for Jim Clifford

1

The Conch

sound   secreted the form,
blew

through the water   its undulant fibers,
breathing the green volutions   and the ivory
of the spiralling vortex.

spoke it!   made it,   its allegro!   twisted the creature
out of the luminous clay   of its tremor!

2

Sound, the progenitor, by continuing to ring through its creation, its forms, begets Speech.

Speech, both the resonance and celebration of Sound.

Speech, that's never pronounced, but *cast, diffused, exuded.*

That communicates with nothing except its own ebullience.

That varies with the depth and contour, the vibratory shell of each form. The iris emitting a different Speech than the dragonfly.

Form, being instrument (as the body on the octaves of its pulsate sensations).

To imagine the fruit, as oboe, and the wind, as bassoon! Blood-harp! Sensations are the fibers of Speech. Are its quills of flowing crystals that, myriad, determine its volume, its intensity, its 'voice.'

Speech radiates *outward*, and aureoles its own energy.

An agony, exuded inwards, submitted, is an inverted Speech. A convulsed exhilaration.

Of all things Spoken, excepting death, love, in its tremor of lust, is the most spacious. And the ultimate motivation of all Speech.

Space, being the efflorescence of Speech. Its circumference.

~

What is *said* is only the glowing residue of what is Spoken: the silage of the ecstatic presence.

Language, that originates in Speech, being reduced to a system of semblances, symbolic equivalents that can only obscure—and no longer instigate, assume—its existence.

Constant and successive repressions having pillaged the original magic of language, and neutralized the immense power of its crystals.

Having cleaved the light, and isolated the voice from its colossal drama. Imposing a communication, an anti-Speech, that conveys everything but its own reality.

Language remains Speech, remains power (springing translucent out of its source) only when uttered with a *total intent.* When it's the flesh that proffers it.

When the breath commits itself to the crystals that it breathes.

As sometimes with the whisper, the green sigh, the jagged shriek.

Or whenever the ode is a rich, glittering secretion.

Where the word-crystals rise in a charged and radiant energy-cluster. A blossoming ellipse.

Where they generate the exact substance they invoke.

Each thing defining itself not by its form, but by its resonant discharge, the spacious aura it exudes, its dynamic circumference.

Where, as Speech, in reaching the ring of this circumference, its diaphanous membrane, it luminously *resounds.* Where Speech, itself, *replies.*

For the imperative of Speech is to hear itself: hear itself *realized.*
As the red concerto, stunned in the shower of its magnificence.

Where, reverberant, the creature is englobed in its own magnitude: the element of both its origin and its most spacious impulsions.

~

Psalms of the leopard and the phosphorescing mosses! Flesh in the wisdom of its crystals! What if heaven (its vast dilapidated structure) were never more than the resonant colossus of each creature? Of each ion? As the opulent sphere that envelops the earth, the earth's Speech, in the skin of a celestial echo.

ALTAMIRA

beast that I love,   breath
      that I slay,

it's the slow green lightning of
   your eyes
      that I see through.

it's my blood, its   wild echoes,   I eat!

GIANT

whipped himself   into magic,   into
whiteness

(then lay in   the luminous fleece
          of his giant's
breath   and breathed
                                        his hunger).

TWICE

        the blue earth
balances in   the mind, and the   mind
        in the muttering flesh: the spirit   somatic.

see how its   words: smoke   and wind,
coil ragged through the plump rusting grapes. . . .

~

the long   resinous body
        lying, motionless, the length of   mine;

limbs,
lips, and
        the thick liquid in the sun's   swift ash.

HELIX

Dawn
diamonds the wind.

Alive.
Alive,
and risking ourselves
on reaching
the Inevitable.

Thighs, boulders, lightning,
we're deep pods
of breath
breathing ourselves
into light.

My teeth; your shoulders.

Flesh
in the throe of its flower,
the air's
spiralling meadow's,
our radiance
is what the wind-crystals sing,
and the black earth
echoes.

NOTES FROM AN ORCHARD

had entered the orchard,
the full ice, the blue celestite
of the flowering orchard.

are there words wide, violent enough to realize
our own innocence?

~

risked myself
in the deafening splendor: the blood,
the harped blood of these inviolate branches
that soar
quilled, through silence.

~

a bee
carves their cold, nubilous mass, adding

its octave. no poles, dialectics in enormity; only
these raw, threading vibrations: aimed
adamant into themselves.

~

something,
within me, was being waged. the vestige bones
of a lost voice.

the last
and first wrestlers.

~

we're not inhuman enough to hear   what we hear   (to
touch   what, craving, we feel).

~

o bliss, its hideous tangle.   the ammoniacal   float.

Inferno
was what we'd made of it,
and shredded the   echo   of these worded-limbs,
the bough   euphoric, that   we couldn't   ravish.

~

be
swift.   in the wind the flowers phosphorescing thicken.

something in me   that isn't mine
would touch the chord

and shatter the rings that   rib me in this ear
of   darkness.

THAT WIDER

Arose.
Against the wind in glassy wheels and the shivering of the sycamores. Stretched in their rich spindles.
To enter. Forever press. The breath forced. The skin new.
The new vowels, mumbling with roots.
With branches.
With birds gliding into their own shadows.

That enter, clamoring.

That wider. Into the white landscapes that forever lessen.

HELIX

The edge,
the edge yields.

Splintering minerals of pure light,
the flesh
lunges fluent
into its blue, euphoric showers.

Its kisses
thrash.
Its beautiful tongues
swim through.

The millennium's ending
in a lucid scroll of hair.

The mirage,
its shattered cage, sings.

And loving,
all the cold elements mesh
in prisms
that oscillate, and flare.

ALL OCTAVES SIMULTANEOUS

for Rhiannon

Saw earth as eventual.

Saw each thing in its dumb, ecstatic solitude.

Cold dawn. Swift wrists.

Out of an underworld came, carrying her lantern of burning seeds.

Word's germinal spin: its helix.

Billow the arms, the hair, out of the breathing words.

Speak until the lizard sings. Until the wind's dagger glows.

Breath-of-life, as language.

As the eye opens, the star grows; as the tongue touches, the flesh blooms.

A form forever wider than the widening dissolutions.

Shook the wind free of its red shrubs.

Detaching, gathered.

Only elation, in its cryptic waves, is coalescence, is wisdom.

Became the other the instant morning became me.

All the glassy fruit, wrestling free.

Blow out of the oboes of genesis, the shivering ions.

Live the length, the thirst of this white vibration.

Larks, through the siphon of their voices, soar.

The soil searches for the eye of the searching root.

Perspective, in its cubes, the length of its verb, will collapse, at last, into its deepest orchard.

Not writing, but waiting; waiting for the recurrent miracle: the breath in the eclipse of its bones.

Was at the earth's edge, gathering sound.

Lay, feeling the entire length of the wind, its iridescence, within me.

Suffered the bliss of each finger.

In the long hesitation of a rock, watched its slow tendons meditate.

Creation risks itself on a harp of red clay.

In the midst of voluptuous space, a metaphor has encaged us.

Crouched for the immaculate leap.

The magpies scatter the sun. Feed it on dragonflies.

The dreams were real: were viscous windows looking out onto ourselves who were already other.

Was looking for their voices (where I'd found, in a pear orchard, a circle of flint tools).

Feeling the emptiness, I gave it its name. Repeated its syllables, over and over, until it formed, in successive tissues, a sphere, a sound-sculpture, standing within the vacated air.

Not the things, but the blissful filament that runs, oscillating, through them.

Our least words *walk* in one another's dreams.

Wind, whose iris we are. Whose stutter.

What you say, said the Voice with the green, momentary eyes of an oak, is what you hear: hear me saying.

Scribbled, and a wall of light, furiously vertical, rose.

Had begun equalling ourselves: begun dying into our own inconceivable beauty.

Each word is already *edged* with new earth.

Off the breath's blue spools unravel the planets.

The mud guttural, the mosses whistling, where a single step, the boot's bristling crystals, crams the universe.

The earth-rock still reverberating in the axe, held upright in the dark air.

Deep down, the kisses dream.

The ring of the lamp is forever wider than its reflections.

The eyes, clamped shut, squeeze to a star.

The lover is the beauty of the beloved.

We're alive between two echoing boulders of vast blackness.

This is, that wasn't: a sprinkling of words in the wind's humus.

The future forever *returns*.

Ends in inception: a grief spawning its small fist of white shadow.

So dark only the light was visible.

Pollen is its own godhead.

EOTOTO

(*song*)

We're earless.

It's the earth
that hears,
the earth,
the earth
that has ears.

That sucks at our voices,
draws us,
sperm-sprig-syllable,
into the echoing whorl
of its rings.

Labyrinth
where the peach tree ripens
and the sputtering planets curl,
for you,
— it's yours —
this wind-rattle sings.

II

Mirrorhead

(1975)

HELIX

The mist burns
to a bronze whisper.

Fields
are the dense, inverted
facets
of a glaucous star.

I taste
and exhale them.

Wind's skin.
Where space,
into its chrysalid, contracts.

Amongst
its breathing minerals
I recognize
my mirror.

Lip.
Lips,
and the blind spine's
bright
shiver.

EFFIGY: ULTIMATELY, THE SISTER

forced beyond   me (through
                    the   illegible light);
forced to   find: to   imagine the
    image
that might   imagine me;
that might,
    replying (in   degrees
            of increasing   density),
    restitute and

    return me.

~

    return, and   rename me.

    for what I am
    would be made out   of castings, of
each word's
    inversion,
            as a breath
beating against the air's   bright metal
    would make of it   its effigy.

~

effigy. the burning surfaces
            at each instant's   extremity.

            the echo-sheets.

for even the infinite
would crease, and the infabled bodies touch,
touch, and rubbing,
mould themselves,

invent themselves
in the wet wavering mirrors of the other.

~

the path
would ride backwards, and the least stones
star and interpret me.
the hills, within, and the hidden trees
would issue, surrounding me in the ring
of their fresh releases.

pure twin
of contrariety. dark sister
in the still drifting chrysalis of sleep,
the image,
the beautiful limbs of the unbidden image,
blown through, and beyond me,
would resound. and my voice, refracted,
would at last reply,

touched by its own incestuous sounds.

MONSTROUS ANGELIC

dawn   dissolves into rocks,   veins
    of wheat.   while the   dream
still juts,
effuses a monstrous softness   that

crawls in the wind with its
                    white scratches.

BREATH VEGETAL

all verbs, verbs of   unravelling.
all light, a
darkening   into ripeness, a ripening
upon the tall   transparent stem.

slipped crystals, and the
warm wind-   pitted suns; and the lips   parting

as the long hair   spreads,
in wet   bracelets, over   the arms.

MAKING THE MIRROR

Mirror, my first light, my darkest mineral.

Nothing I say, but that I'm said; nothing I touch, but that I'm touched.

For each thing: its breathed equivalent: its spatial counterweight.

The tongue-cast anatomy of the other: the errant twin.

No way of seeing you without astonishing myself.

Presence is tension: tension with an absence that, elsewhere, is equally present.

For the archer, only the interval is sacred.

It's the breath-crystals alighting that constitute the mirror.

We were not meant to be saved, but to seize and be seized by intense identities.

Writing: to temper myself against a surface of living replies.

Nothing in the thing, but the thing reflexive: in its own dialectical echo.

Bend the flaccid glass of the light. Make it your bow.

It's the beloved, within us, that becomes the poem.

Perilous throne of a voice. Its voices.

The mirror, vanishing; its fugitive reflections.

Age of eaten effigy.

A path is gasping at a cloud.

A land has elapsed, unfabled, unhappened.

Five days in the imageless city — blazing heart!

Pain answers pain; makes a luminous appeal to power.

The minuscule, utterly magical cleavage within the body.

To split the instant and create an interlude, a moment of historic evasion into which our entire life could rush.

Luminous chairs!

To feel, finally, the tree, touching my finger.

It's by what we didn't see that we'll recognize ourselves.

Spread hands glorying against the gushing source.

The force flowing against us is also ours.

PORCELAIN

    enough
    of each of us   isn't
to beg of the   other: our   echoing whiteness;

to see, through the bunched   iris, beyond us,
    our fluid   star (grown   even whiter)

floating against the   wind-walls of the light.

BOTH

pulls light out of stone.
pulls smoke that ripples like skins,
gildings over the eyes,

that warps
the minutes,
makes love to the dark heart that delivers it.

HELIX

Susanna's

Listen,
the two mirrors
touch.
Rasped
their glowing surfaces sing.

In them
the rivers
and the clotted orchards
bunch.

Skin
springs,
but their ground breath beats
against an irreducible light.

The ovals
only
echo.

Milled winds.
Inviolate dust.

Their dense vowels
drain
into night.

AS THE INSTANT CEASES

(Sami-Ali)

this,   that isn't,
is the white pressure
of a slowly   diminishing instant,
the intricate collapse of   its distances.

is its hills, in glass   facets, drawn inwards,
as the cubes of a   protracted earth
converge: in
stuttered increments   coincide.

~

in stutters, the spasms of   a luminous skein . . .

for the breath   magnetizes the
elements that it   names, and sucking at the   wind's
fibrous quartz (the breath,
the entire body in the rooted-leaves of   its breath)
assumes the space that its   saying expiates.

old crimes of   an obliterated age
still wandering through the cold   hypnotic rocks. . . .
archaic expulsions,
projections,
irretractable stars.
the word draws, swarming, at   the scattered word;
the   fingers,
moving as   lures
through the furiously   abstracted air,   grope
for the fingers, the   hands
that once felt themselves as   another's,
voiced in the other's   indissoluble caress.

the instant clatters.
the   turret, over the   black meadow,
writhes.

the voyage
contracting into   its alveole of
echoless   immensity
hears, at last, the   vessel of   its own breathing.

the mirror creases.   the beloved   speaks.

a tongue is   tracing the flesh as the instant
ceases.

CHAPLADE: SUMMER

1

came back, breath-
thinned,
from milking shadows.

the other
whirred,
wouldn't listen
to its tongue,

rotated
without me.

2

heard me   in the sudden abyss, the feather-
headed reeds
where your long body   flickered:

the flint, kissing the shadow that   it kills.

3

a breeze   blows from the forehead . . .

the same
extravagated body   receives it: the gift
of interval: its   perfect line.

the curls open, the
shadows   clatter: are small   black sticks.

ISAIAN

disks of wind — scoopings!

dust.
dust in each finger's throat, as the hands
    murmur the weeds,
thrash
at the grain's sudden spectral lamps (their
    holocaustic gold).

dust.
dust and dreams,
    and this blazing grain
that bends the eye
    and forces the white breath to feed.

TWO

the halves
can't hear.   is why the flesh   pounds so
            and closes

the lashes of   the honeysuckle.

~

in the last   field, where the   deep eye
is altar,
                        a last stone
                  is stammering another.

TERRA ALBA

in the direction
of a vanishing:

sudden terraces and
a leaf
the length of the tongue.

~

know you
by the glow of   your voice:
amber, elastic, chimerical; by

the flight of   its splinters in the cypress-hedge.

~

you pointed the way, and
the wind
suddenly entered.
someone (was it you?)
was sitting, skirt spread,
beneath an oak,
reading
the white calendar,

~

my gaze creases,
returns
in the instant's wet
windfallen
globe,

your gift
faceted
to my fingers.

IDYL

Our eyes
were entering
the last islands.

The alphabet
of the waves,
of the leaves
lay bleaching.

Each
the risk
of the other,
we sipped at the long
phosphorescing quill:
its single tremor.

Was the breath netted
in the netherlight?
Could the white reefs hear?

Around us,
all morning,
even the bees
seemed breasted.

Our hands spilt
the matted space
of a murmur.

SEVEN PERSEIDS

the first   squirts white, accelerating.   dissolves
      into the same   dissolving instant;
                                                            the eye

scarring the heart
    with the long-tailed ash of   its light.

~

another,
plummeting softly (a pale lime)
ploughs
the
black; troughs it
to a greater black.

a slow flint   turning
to a sulfureous tear.

~

          my breath,   riding the back: the   breath
of the blown   petroleum star: a

    pure verb and the   shadowing sperm
    of its fire.

~

how the tail   chases the head: reaches it
    as they rush, simultaneous,
                into extinction.

a wisp.
a twinged   wire that
    throbs, through   the black heavens,
                gelatinous.

~

    the ephemeral   instant,
an instant   late.   the rushed dark,   inseminated.

        (nothing, not even
    the charred feather,   was wasted).

~

            we look back
on the black   vaulted magma,
on a space we've never, entirely, come   free of . . .

ancestral flames, and their long   awesome relics:
        flares
              consuming themselves: the length
of the rib's
fixed wonder.

~

    the air
has swallowed its fires.   earth, again,   unravels:
    a wind   spindled to a stone.
    my daughter stirs; first light
is catching,
is   pearling through her hair.

FOSSILIZED LIGHT: FRAGMENTS

. . . for the stars first erupted
from beneath the skin, and
rose in luminous incrustations: warts
of flaming sulfur
and spark-headed carbides;
and the fire was painless, then,
and quenching,
for the darkest spaces, the mind's deepest cryptology,
thrived entire
on the glittering, pulsate surface of things;
and all matter and combinations of matter
existed simultaneous in a
vast cellular weave: a Vision,
Empedoclean: a meshing without depth,
identity or dimension.

~

and between us, shooting in fingers and
long liquid limbs,
a blowtorch of
turquoise continuously breathed.
and there was no way of touching one another
without touching, tasting, sucking at oneself;
(as your nipples soared, and
stabbed florescent, my tongue would become them,
and our entire bodies would lapse and twine
and interchange).

and bathing in the green sheathing liquids
of our own flames,
you'd touch what I'd hardly thought, conceived,
for all thoughts were things or the process,
instantaneous, of becoming things:

wind-glyphs, sculptures of
intense volatility, bolts that spasmed
to a glowing nerve, a bone, a breathing tree.
and time, too, was matter
and poured erratic, without sequence, like
long hair undulating through a dark oil. . . . . .

~

this, though,
was before the breath was gutted, and
the stars
lanced and jettisoned into cloven space.

was before the body
became this catacomb of howling flesh, and
flesh, the amnesia of its own
auroral intelligence.
(we were already living in the clay of these baked
still- cooling mirrors).

was before even the birth of lust
when lust would leave us with words; only words
to re-weld
the dissipated elements.

words,
and the brute, ecstatic cells
that could still, occasionally,
echo an integer . . . . . .

HOLD FLOWING POLYPHONOUS

The last men mumbling under the earliest trees.

The ground is engendered.   Meaning fumes.

The first words: words of clay, fleece, bark.

The Was and Would Be are linked: are exhilarant.

A red flickering of language beneath the earthen jars.

The field, the dawn's, tilts toward me; its cold planets spill.

Each hill: a held breath.

In unnaming myself, accumulated space.

The words: dark stones scattered at the boundaries of light.

Beads of thirst!

Even grief, this morning, is malleable: is only a thing for making other things.

Grinding the dead images to a germinal dust.

Our transit is lexical.

Made love like moths; awoke without recognizing ourselves.

Each finger undreams us.   Frees us of our furious spelling.

The meadow enters its marigolds; the body, its glowing tongues.

To dwell in a space chiseled with whispers.

Everything finally converges, is confluence, but only at the peripheral.

Substance flees.

The curves of thirst: their obscure geometry.

Was two hoofs of breath and a dry stutter.

Was a mouth in a gray marsh, feeding on glints.

Time, the black breeze, punctured the air.

Saw the souls as dark, gracefully spinning relics.

All of us caught in the earth's deaf honey.

There must be intervals between the pebbles.

Between each instant, a white needle.

The page as surface: as a field of conciliations.

Each thing reflects, but only the word contains.

Mountains are the weightless games of our voices.

To inhale myself; to hollow out a density.

To feed myself to my words.

Spend the night, talking to rocks.

The breath cleanses itself in blackness.

Everything had to close before the breath-calyx could open.

Ephemeral metals! Reality was our last mask!

A silence is clashing ponderously with sound.

The fingers shall touch, and the names change.

Only love would be light enough to support such weightlessness.

Beyond the ring of questions, the first unprecedented answers shall alight.

Miniscule fruits of the thunder!

It's thirst that sculpted the source.

THE TWO FACES OF LIGHT

clashed
with light.

came back branded
by its serene
alluvial
face,

while the other,
the darker,
the ashless,

plummeted
even deeper.

LA GIOVANETTA

(Titian)

Your eye
icons
the dark blaze
that it makes:
its spined
nimbus
of loose
oscillated
rays.

Gray
wondrous
muscle:
star
where my body
swims,
thrives magnified
through its long
bronze-lashed
gaze.

Around you
the winds
in raw curtains
thicken;
the deep pigments
crease.
Neutral,
magnificent,
you draw
the wild
siphoning cells
into your instant
that isn't.

Iris,
archaic
obsessor,
I swarm
swelling
into this mirror's
inversion:
black logos
of a pure
irreflection.
Alveole,
where the earth
would flake,
the air
fly,
the self
vanish
toward
some immeasurable
reply.

Whose
are your hands?
The rich wave of your thigh?
Innocent,
nullifying,
yours is the light
no breath-light
divides.
Over your shoulder,
in the bowl
of a meadow,
sheep,
in thick scrolls, graze,
fixed, already,
in the aura,
the transfiguring gold
of your gaze.

CHAPLADE: AUTUMN

1

always the same breath, boots,   whistles
      in the wind-clotted   orchard;

   backwards and   forth, being equal.

always the cold   lashes of shadows,   the
   hole where the   words went,

the hands
tapping at the edge, waiting for the   hands'
   answers.

2

   comes back
      with each small, stuttered   particle
still whirring.   goes out, comes back,
   is   in the same instant: another;

   while wanting to live;
   while wanting a   name to live in.

THE WEIGHTS

to John

lay
these weights into   the light,
                              that they won't

                              dissolve (dream-trinkets
of the clay, the darker   light's).

that among the rabid
     rotating images (all
                              we'd ever seen of   ourselves)

                              the lapidated
                              may chant,

                              may lift   them.

TOWARDS

. . .par la découverte d'un troisième terme. .

the twins,
in half-turns,
grind
at the green pebbles,
their syllables;

rise, unwheeled,
without realizing,
arm-spoked
over the opening
oils.

HELIX

Wasp
autumn.
The gold's
rotting
in the long winds;
the tips of the fingers fume.

Who'll know
the orbits
of the new hours,
the brown-haired wheels
of their hymns?

The grape-
crates thunder.
And through the weather's
ear
the root
transluces.

Our faces
fuse.
The vines
ignite.

Into
a bloom
of intricate feathers
the full dusk
blazes.

BREATH'S REFLECTIONS

1

wanting to say what I'd hear,
wanting to say
what it is that I wanted to hear,

(while moving, wordless, through the white
weightless shell,
reading shadows,

nudging rocks).

~

wanting to say;
wanting to hear
what it is that I wanted to say.

since hearing
was what I was,
was what it was that enveloped me
in the ear of an enveloping ellipse.
what held me
while space
chanted wheeling, through the black chambers
of each cell,
and heard itself heard in

the hearing I was,

as I was the space,
as I was what it was I heard.

~

words
aren't enough; are the attempt at words;
are what words, generating themselves,
would say.

but saying, first, is reaching; is reclaiming
the breath
that the breath cleaved: its
ruptured expanse:
its land
of doubles, of dissolving echoes,
where the circles
search for their edge: rim
where the rock would quiver,
and each word
reappear, ribbed in its magnitude.

~

for saying, in itself,
says nothing. saying
is the breath, in the shred of its syllables,
thrust, projected
against space's
mirrored extremity:
the tissue of each breath in its entity.

where
the body, being named,
would resound,
would feel itself slowly enveloped
in the arms and hair,
in the luminous hands of its own hearing,

hearing itself in the same word as its saying;
hearing itself said
in its hearing.

2

who are you (who was, once,   myself);
who are you
                    who'd listen,
                    who'd   hear?
(who was, once, the   girl whose   eyes burnt,
          tugging at her scarf of   cerulean stars).
what
would   contain, what membrane   withstand
          this torch of   nerve,
          the blown fibers of   a saying, of   a life
inside the   inflamed tongue
          of a saying,
                              that says   nothing.

who are you,
who,   being touched, would touch and
          touching, would withhold the   instant,
        the word in its   infinite accretion,
                              would withhold it, and   hear.

~

wanting to say,
wanting to say the   eyes
        in which   the eyes would, at last, resound,
        and each limb,
                              reflect;
(where
          projection, in its lost orchards, replies).

who are you,
who are you   who's breathing through me?
        whose hair   braids itself in   my breath?
who still   wordless
is waiting in   shimmers

for your name to   name me,
and to wrap yourself,
a new   creature, in the   flesh of   your mirrors.

Celebration of the Sound Through

I

Wave's Scaffolds

(1977)

CAESURAE: MIDSUMMER

rides the line of myself outwards (the

measure) to a
first ripple's

return.

---

reduces air
to
this handful of
sounds,
thrives
vibrant inside it,
survives
the
white
wind-flaked
relic, be-
yond.

. . . . dark
for the long eyes
drawing
their chalk
through.

---

all summer
emptied the
hills (as if
something
less than my
hands
would
reach you).

---

you never knew
you
were me;
you

never were.   walked in
and out
of your own
inappeasable
eye; weren't

even
you.

---

was no
room white
enough to
catch
this:
this
lightning,
your
fabulous
lash.

---

it came up, off
your face, filled
everything.

---

the quick
of the wind: the wind's
gold isn't
what we
thought, is
exactly what
we've never
thought, is
why the ruins in
the high hills
crouch so
in-
side it.

---

myself:
my
eyes-in-leaves, keeping

the mind
mindless,
alert,
away from the
hive
where the
halves

might
touch.

---

coming
down
even brighter.   light rising
from
each finger, over
the eyes, out
onto the

slope.

---

an
alphabet
of glass
let-
ting what it
says (its
clay
instants)
come
through.

---

quicker: that
nothing
be lost (that al-
ready in
the gray surf, be-
yond our own eyes'
evasions,
we
could catch glimpses
of ourselves).

---

white waves
moving
over black (bone-

lines
of the mind).

---

as if
a
sacrifice in
the name
of the
null, that

swollen
light, its
liquidity,

sent
across.

---

no way
away
from

me, other
than

you, you
moving
out-

side your-
self, be-

yond
your white

replies.

WHERE

only words could
catch words: keep them (our-
selves inside them) from the flagellant whir,

from being wingbeaten into the else,
the ever-
extracting where.

TRAJECTORY

wakes

to a wall; an
eye
squiding

across
it.   blow-
ing

other
eyes: lives
over
the riddled lime.

limbs
that cast

and dripping
through their
thick
vitreous
hair,
would hold the

eye; with-
hold the

instant
that's driving the

eye
end-

lessly
over.

ASH

what the ash
whirled through my ear: that you're
the token you'd need, the
voice-bone,
crossing
these eviscerated waves.

SAMU

the whole thing: for carrying   forward, the
fire that's
stacked
against your shoulders, the   no-

body's name in its bright updraft of   shadows . . .

VOICE

voice
that the voices
couldn't feed on.   the iris
of the wine
wrinkling
in a

tall breeze, the
terraces
pressed through the lids . . .
love,

this swollen lamp
you've
dressed in
has deepened.   a

myrrh
of nerves
curls through the tendons:
trellises.
trap

of octaves!   whispers
beating
against bone!   a breath-

threading breath
through all the
amber that
pours
over the long-winged boulders.

WITNESS

watches the   rock (as if

the rock   would last,
would outlast his   eyes, watching it,

wasn't bleaching in   his eyes, as   white

as his   eyes).

NEITHER THIS. . . .

neither this: this tracking, the
scribbles lost
in the breath-prints of the tracking,
nor anything
else, other,
out-
side of this . . . .

ANIMALIAN EVE

night was   and
wisteria: was   your name (anima-
lian Eve) that scattered the panicking
words, that they'd
hold
these star-
squinted heavens   together.

SAINT PANTALÉON

lets the
eyes   out: those tall
wind-tombs, that   your own voice   catch you
   (over the tops
of the clotted figtrees) in quick
successive creases.

ODE

for Charles Tomlinson

1

were saying these things to   stop them,

to   keep them   from
being said by   the ceaseless (the un-

sayable).

~

held,   holding them: the breath's gold:
Rembrandt's

black
elephants.   because luminous   is
what we've learnt to   darken   (to
circumscribe) with   sound: hoop
to this
circus
of   inversions.

~

images.   tokens and
images:

all   we know; that we'll ever   know of
ourselves.   im-

prints of an
obliterating
as-
cendency (fingers
poking

over the coils of the   fuming kelp).

~

what
we call holiest
goes under.   whatever's
ours is

only ours
against.

in crypts
of whispers,
mud-
hovels, our white   chords
hoarded; all
our bright-winged
demons
ballasted
in   blood.

2

all   we know; that we'll ever know . . . .

but the flare, the
clamoring
flue of
the
limbs, up-
wards . . . . lovelier
than anything
we've   ever known.   the lessening
into immensity,   the spreading   trees
of the instants
in bud.   each worded   circle, re-

lapsing, trans-
lucent, into the   eye-
alleviant
of   loss.

~

we'll never   say
what we'd   say.   the jealous   soil, its
syntax,
keeps us doubled to our-
selves.   a voice-net

shrivels us
in its   chimeras.

but the sense,
forever,
swells outwards.   the null,
sumptuous, draws   at the divided voice.

hear the
intervals
as they pour through the   comb of their
octaves; and the   words,
boned
of   all but their   breath,
spread
radiant.

~

was why
he   turned.   why

startled, out-
raged, she stopped.   and felt her   rip-
pling tall-hipped body
dissolve
to a
word.

wings.

wings!   all we have   instead of   wings!

ARCHAIC

. . . can never overcome what you've forgotten,
but fill, could
fill the invisible with your hardest facets
(shadow crystals); casting
what you couldn't hold
onto those warped heavens you'd never touch.

PHRASINGS

pure wound, the white   earth earlier, e-
qual.   its hills
                no   higher than its meadows.

---

   the bees   locked
in all that wisteria, the   cool fume of its

   cones   (hallucinatory dungeon).

---

   later
came the first   mirrors: the frail   breath-
combs.

---

     everything said: said in-   stead of.

---

puz-
zling thunder.   o-
pen

vocable.

---

there's that.   only
that, and it's   nothing, you say, squint-
    ing into it,   nothing,
nothing at   all.

---

turning the twig of a   word: releasing its

silences.

---

the Things,
the   Things, in be-
    tween the words, ex-   ist.   peer through.

the locked bodies nighted, *neithered* to
themselves.

it's the eye that sculpts the apple, feasts

on its white peelings.

tense projections: at each instant: retractable.

only this hand to
hold you, its un-
ringed fingers, letting go.

even here at the very
edge, even this to be opened, emptied,
chanted free
of it-
self.

---

depth, the

mouth (the unsoundable island).

---

to chase your name
down into darkness: to capture its

amnestic glints.

EROS METONYMIC

in and
in: as if, from under the   images: rises . . . .

CA' D'ORO

bulbed
out-
wards, the
imbarcadero
len-

ses the
senses.   water-
cut, the words
slip

through.   your
world, in those
immense

muscles of
hair, the lime-
green linens
you travelled with.
once

still is.   the
heavens

unravelled.   on a
wrist,

over the taut
rocked water, the
white barge

pivots.

LAGOON

saw
in that cloud
of   sound the tall   turbaned poles, the
            churned markers that

the mouth, counting,   spelt outwards. . . .

THE HUT

for letting go   of.   catch-
flow.   making the
                    little hut (the voice-hovel) of the
un-
inhabitable.

WHO

as if who
were hidden inside a where, a
where-cage (edgeless, wind-scored) that the
thighs, without
touching, pearled through . . .

WAY

are given the distances, the tenses: toward.

to move through everything you'd ever let go of.

flowering masks!

were worshipping the word you couldn't interpret.

wild, luminous, serene: that eye that's blowing through you.

. . . through the breezeroots.

'nothing' was never 'no one.'

were: what you moved towards against your own oncoming replies.

lavish eliminator: liminal Eve.

through the sparkling wastes, those lupine angels, extending the scaffolds of space.

chasm-weeds.

a heart, honking at nothing, treading air, guessing at itself.

was still what you didn't know to guide you: its light, like a luminous clay, to unearth.

why the dragonflies moored, immobile, over the drifting instant.

leasting air to those sudden beads.

letting the words take you towards wherever they'd come from.

a mouth: for rooting in.

what pulled you toward it, and touched, like an iris, only itself.

. . . had a name; had only a name.

sperm-let, that it couldn't be told, but continuously shuttle, like a blank money, a frenetic stillness.

were setting yourself to sound.

scaled heart!

wedging the air to its white alphabets.

to sleep in the face you'd never reach: the light of the face you'll never return from.

A WAVE, FLAKING. . . .

a wave, flaking   rose: rush
of the tissues   forward: that you'd carry,
carry their shattered image into the   invisible;
stand, ankles rung, in
the cold flow.

PASTORALE

        was autumn
                        in its bled metals.   who,
again, was   with you,
was the clear wound you   moved through, the

lens of the meadows the   last bees seeded . . .

DIADEM

finally the   eye enters: is (among
the low walls and dark   tufted junipers)
angel to its own   luminosity.   the
lamp and   illegible letter   that

burns in the wind to the   very edge of its fingers.

WRITTEN IN THE RINGS

(*Catullus 11*)

wrung in
wild

drops, Noah's
breath-
threaded waves, wave-
cells, numb-
er us out-

wards.   un-,

un-
to their *tunditur unda*,

who,
whose: the
bled
salts, the boned surf.

in,
uttered, through the
cracked
tabernacle, where the
strings
would mingle and
maze and
wed.

II

Nenuphar

(1980)

LEIS ESPAVENTAUS

for Jolaine

there, rattling
in their bright   plastic tatters: semblance
    as semblance, the
earth's
                        last lamps.

---

or on strings, dangling   from cane, tiny fist-
fuls of
        tinsel.

---

only the mute's trans-
lucent (pulling us through
those white idling harlequins,
its rickety up-
drafts of current).

---

was no one (so
close); a thump of jugs on its cross-staves.

---

then one
that wasn't one: rigid, minute, over the foaming
breeze-clipped surface of the grain, *la*
devinaira, reader of
residues and
vapor.

---

through a dead man's
washed smoke-   white sleeves, is whistling out . . .

---

or, across a pale gauze, the
sprouted onions', this angel of   the seeds, hat-

deep, drowning in a   nimbus of flowers.

---

shrimp-

pink the scarves   skirts billow out, over the

makeshift
scaffolds, while the
gaze, your   mirrored gaze (*madòna*
d'ombra) squints
gold.

TROUBADOUR

what I love's the
squander, to
spend
and spend, through the
cold air 'run

with the pennants,' as if
world

were still
to be reached, wrung from its
mirrors: wind, gypsum,
brushweed,
all

those des-
olate metals.   its
meanings
breached, blown

through. . . .you'd
turned

to a distance.   with-
in you (the skirt, the
pearl of
your skirt spreading, like a *resonance*,
an *element*) I'd risen.
routes

of Provence, smoke
in drafts through the black cypresses . . .
'there's this, this,' you
tell me.   as the

fingers open, they're
filling
with curls.

SHADOW RATTLES

(I)

~

what the eye flies after trans-
luces; what
you want, doesn't want: it vanishes. . . .

you're only yours, mutter and
muscles, as you enter it, its vanishing.

~

sound, too (the cricket ticking
in dry grass) cracks light. 'out, out, out,'
you'd written,
your only
where.

~

we're almost not, and
know it. but the poem, the poem happens
before us, and we send it across, in-

nocent and still hesitant, instead of us.

~

(Simiane-la-Rotonde)

in bowls
of glowing wind, bristles   violet.   look,
how you
look, turn   thirsting towards . . .   but
already, in its

breath-
beaten mirrors, the stacked lavender   burns.

~

then, suddenly, you stood there and
I couldn't
believe it.   I pretended it was you, and that

you stood there, and was me that you gazed at.

~

(the image)

this breeze (I can't keep it, wouldn't
wish to) blows   out onto your face . . .

I touch you, make sure that it's there.

~

mirror-
less except for this: those gray eyes, their
quick slip sideways. . . . .

~

draws us, that
dim
residual pearl (anywhere, would go anywhere
to reach it,
to dissolve in that light that's outside of us).

~

(*the hoe*)

were words: for turning it, a black loam
of imponderables (those,

at least, you could call yours, and
the rage, the
lie rising up from the rage
to substantiate the leaves, the living. . .)

~

the real's with-
out.   but   wedged into our white
releases,
we irrigate the light, the very   light that's denied us.

~

nothing, finally,
was worthier than the grief that forced the   question,
the earth-
hooded worder   forwards.

~

light again, and then
gone.   in the
wobbling
word-
pitted hollow (writing, you said,
that you wouldn't
be written) the
real, un-
remittent grace of the impossible.

THUS

from there, the
wave's

tiny,
ruffled, like
a doll's sleeve.   we're
feeding

on so little, sip-
ping breath
out of

whispers, signs, the
story that's
hidden, em-
bedded, in another ('*can't*

be told, can
never. . . .').   but

glints
through the twin windows,
ripples

gold
where the mouth, once,

broke open.

FLOWERING CHERRIES

~

up through their
gray   oily torsos (in weight-
less waterfalls of   light) is earth-the-word
that's lifting, re-
leasing the   earth, letting

it out.

~

the eye, by
itself, would go on   and on.   but *there*, the
flying meat, in those   sudden
vermilion instants, shatters and   replies. . . .

(like the petals, blown
in out of   where you'd been moving towards).

~

wasp-hearted, their bracelets
of cold coral-   white blossoms, are what
you'd written: that   heap

of shadows you're   telling yourself to. . . .

~

a madrigal
of branches. off the lowest (flowing
    ruffled, like a chopped current) the
badger
will be feeding—lunarian—on the pigeon's heart.

~

only *visible* to yourself in the instant that
that phosphor vanishes (through the
  tendons of the cherry: the quills, in the
wake of the quills, alive in their annihilating
                    updraft).

~

luenh es lo castelhs

like threads, the
petals, in the lee of the deep ruts, run
    on and on. . . . . 'never'

was what those wind- broken jugglers meant.

SPRING: AN EXTRAVAGANCE

one mouth
blows into another.
both

have grown on the
white fats
of the petals; we

weight-
lessly open . . . let
one another

out. nowhere
is what's around.
we turn and

touch, as if
one of us — the other —
were still there.

DRAFT: FOR SANTA CRUZ

1

spoke, but couldn't
say (what
it was, sound's

empty
yet preponderant thing:
as if

to stand here, in near-
spring, before the
first

squirting vineshoots, the
earth, still a death-
hoof, a no-

head, to say 'me,' to
be: depended on
the clatter

of those dry un-
substantiated syllables.
look, here's a

leaf, and
there: there's another . . .
'leaf' breaks — as

I say it — volatilized
between the lips
and teeth).

2

o all
that insistence, that ganging
of stars in-

to a single in-
voluted syntax; such
densities, for

circumscribing what? — a
breath?   '*per-*
mettez-moi d'ex-

primer cette appréhension,
demeure
une incertitude. . . .'

'compose.   (no ideas
but in. . . .)'
grammatik.

3

floats, im-
mobile, in the frieze
of its

ribboning woodsmoke. . .
the village, the
image, the al-

ways *else*
that tells us, tell
us: 'we're here.'   but

the reflection
we've made, and pro-
jected about us, like

some cylinder of
light, is
riddled.   substance

flees.   and through
the breath-
invested intervals, its

blown threads
flare. . . . is ours, what
isn't, what

we've
worked free of the
'here,' and its echoing-

rhetorical 'there.'   are
neither's, the
no-

where's, but this
bright draft
between.

4

'through,'
not 'towards,' was
the word that

took me — each
time — past
myself, and into the

null's
suspended accelerant.
(were others I

knew
who'd twisted wings
out of rags

and arm-
lengths of wire; while
still others, the loveliest,

turned and
turned, and even
in their braided dreams, only

saw blue).

Envoy

'I,' word
that I come upon, happen
in, in this

wind-
beater's language, the
mirror-syllable, *am*

these things
that I've teased forth
into translucence: the sheer

tooth and flower, at
earth's end, the very earth
yet to appear.

SHADOW RATTLES

(II)

~

(ars poetica)

a breath-nail
being beaten into   air (at the   very end
   of numbers, having run
out of earth, water,   light)
                                        this   wedging-where.

~

   are ourselves, turned in-
side   out (it might have been   our deaths we'd
   been talking about, so   careful

how we   touched, told one another   what we did).

~

the secret 'between'
        gets told over and   over, without
ever   being revealed (in white
half-wheels, thins

to these hissing salts,
        and this breath of   ours, ground backwards).

~

are us, the others, except
for those oily shadows that we've cast out over
them (and thus
made love to ourselves, our frail in-
verted vacuity); is image, what

we've moved through
and suffered from, nothing else: from idea, *idealis*.

~

was nothing further, and still moving (wind-
shots, and the
floppy-hatted shadows of the staved vines), to tell:

tell one another what we'd never heard, ourselves;
(while the selves rushed through their bunched wires).

MANDOLINS

. . . chewed
on that
rippling

gold; threaded
it, wet,
to a

tautness.   so
huge
with un-

doings, our
lives (are
what

we'd quickened
into
still-

ness. . . . . had
driven, our
chins

wedged, into
that deep
leaf-

less dark
we're
strung to. . . . .

. . . .
. . . .
. . . .)

lay
there, in a
wave of

white
angles, while
the mirrors

blew
out, over
us, like eyelids.

SUDDEN ESSAYS
ON SHADOWS AND SUBSTANCE

the shadow, within, thinks of itself as substance
        while what it   wishes (the other)
appears as   substance, is only
                        its obliterating reply.

---

        if the shadow points
it's because the   shadow's drawn; drawn, I
        call it 'you,'   'yours,'
                when it's never yours but

the glint you make   that pulls the shadow through. . .

. . . all one's darkness, being weighed,   risked
in those   thin
tin- white quivers.

---

you, because
I didn't want: never asked   for myself,
but slaked, each time,
on your shattered mirrors.

---

under a breeze-cloth of glances, is letting
the light bones   go.

---

if word   is, if
          world is: it's outside *what-*

ever it is that wishes to name, number,   elaborate.

---

          is the shadow-
within-the-   flesh, reflected, that permits passage; is
     nothing before or   beyond it; only
                                        its 'between.'

---

     through the narrows   that
          draft of   fumes, as it thickens
to a murmur: the white   rhyme of its dissolution. . . .

---

filled the world with   ourselves; then, invented a
grail, ir-

resonant enough.

---

the fingers, curling
into claws, to
withhold the   rolled smoke of the shadows (as if

they could).

---

as the fanned lashes   touch: the smoke
cones through.

---

on   and on, one soul
        ridding itself upon   another: our heaven-cir-

cuitous.

---

rushed, each time, towards the
hollowest, the 'heart   of lepers,' this

gift   of our needlessness.

---

awash in those ashes: still talked   of roses. . . . .

---

am the   transparent mask that
you've made: in half-circles, the
wild ash   rubbed into arms, shoulders, your
long   glowing face.

---

to bury our shadows   under the
lashes of
their reflection, is what   we mean; murmur of. . . .

THE CHEVAL GLASS

(*T'ang*)

glances back-
wards, be-

tween the
two
turquoise flamingoes;
fingers

swim to her cheeks,
fork
through
those tossed fires . . .
my

shadows, too, drift
into the image, my
arms take
root

in her sleeves. . . .
so

many cells for that
gray
glowing oval; her
pearls spill,
clicking,

be
tween
its tapering beaks.

BRONZE
An Exercise in Style

(Li Shang-Yin)

1

. . . . our reflections
flaked, like
wraiths,

through the revolving doors . . . .

. . . .

inside, where
the ether bloomed
on its tall icy stems, your
sleeves crushed:

cerulean.
twice,

now, into
nowhere, travelled
on the vaporous back of
our voices.   the
waves

froze.
forever ended.   the
darts, off your gold bow-ring,
flew backwards.

2

‘for so
little,’ the myth.   Prince O piled
the embroidered quilts.
their weights

rolled over, and
opened. . . .
was,

were, lay
soundless
under the shallow gray lightning
of each other’s
lids.

3

a clatter of
shell

against crystal; a dragon, its
wings
riding salient
on a starched wrist. . . .

. . . .

. . . . is world,
what’s

turning again into
voices, waves, the pronged
troughs
of its thick, suspended brocades. . . .
a

rasp
of combs: no
holding . . . . the
heart

shall fly, hooded, the
breath
breaking on its shivering scales. . . .

4

half-

turned, in a
froth
of shadows. . . .mirrored, already,
over the

matched
majolica dogs.

SHADOW RATTLES

(III)

~

. . . . shredded the world apart (for
something that's not even there: the white
heart that
might have inhaled us. . . .)

~

even now that there's nothing, the
dew that the wind bruises rose
holds 'heaven-and-earth'—for an instant—in
this null-
syllabic.

~

the *bodies* are there
to un-
imagine the *selves*: to
ring the insufferable magnitude of the
other-

within-them: work it to a whiteness.

~

had never slept
in my own sounds, but folded the
shadows back over the rippling bed; made

somewhere you might awaken in. . . .

~

charged with the meaning — the lineation
of small gestures (of all things, your
hands, above all else) the poem moves

through the death of its making . . . is death,
its crushed vapors, that keeps it
alive.

~

"*sur Venise, l'hiver…*"

the 'things,' the
heart's foaming particles, have only ourselves, now,

for shattering against.

~

fed on the shadow
of those white mushrooms that the snow coned
even whiter. . . . (world's

for finding what it flies through. . . . .)

VIOLETS

for E. W.

as if, some
form of

ex-
change, for

crossing
my

own
frozen shadows

on, the
worn

toys of the
wrist,

jaw,
groin, what

there
is, for

wagering a-
gainst . . .

~

. . . . . violets,
mud-

stars, my
life's

flickering
amongst

them.   for
less, a

next-
to-

nothing, their
heart-

stops, breath-
holes draw

me (some
ob-

solescing
game

of the
air's), my

white
ice-

scarf
of mumbles.

~

rue,
prunings,

rock thrush,
it's

the syl-
lables we

send, in-
stead of our-

selves . . . (the
eye,

alone, would
fly for-

ever
through the

bit-
ter minerals

of the
light; if it

failed, if
once the

words
were to end).

~ ~ ~

. . . . . being
but

sound, in a
stave

of bone, over
the

mud studded,
gas-blue.

VOLUTES

is always at a distance that the voice
  is fashioned: all words, re-

plies, pronged into the mute- exquisite.

---

that you're there matters, is all
  that matters, those

tense ripples, these immense inventions. . .

---

from a shadow, half-
turned through the wrist: wheat- luminous.

---

density is image: image
alveole (the
channelled mirror- combs of what
we cherish).

---

on and on, on the bone-
white boulevards (are

what we interrupt ourselves with).

---

the 'through' is the fluctuating current of
the real: its riddled *charm* . . .

---

whose voice, even,
was for reading my own eyes by. . .

---

the image: both ob-
durate and transparent,

shattering the very pain that projected it.

(*a note from St. Rémy*)

rhythmic, the tympanum,
into the long refectories of
the mad . . .

~

bite this: this
is the bread of his hair; the irises

weren't out yet.

LAGOON: RELIQUIAE

1

the bones
of

her
fingers, as

if
floating in

their tall
lan-

tern of
crystals. . .

the moon's
too,

her mute
inter-

cessions,
for

winnowing
the clotted

salt
by.

2

waste, at
the

very
center: that

precious
cell. . . . .

~

'wanted
to

fly, no
longer

speak. . . .'
as

if density
held

less: scaf-
folds,

scena, the
blown

voices of
the in-

finitely
iden-

tical . . . .
. . . .

. . . .
shook,

from the
sim-

ulated
lightning,

your brittle
tear.

~

. . . . . wore
blue . . . .

. . . . rings . .
(travelled

as if
past your-

self . . . .
. . . . . tasting

rocks . . . .
. . . . . ash . . .

. . . . the
eyes

of your
own

ob-
fuscations).

. . . .
. . . .

read,
once, in

the palm
of

the waves, the
cracked

letters: *was,*
wasn't,

world
blew through.

The Earth as Air

I

At the Flaked Edges

MADRIGAL

with you
what I know of

the world
opens, has

that of
swelling, wave as

it tatters, a
ruled line, against

reefs, a
breadth that

still
spreading, breaks

in-
to dull tokens, spent

petals, what the
poem

would
close on, hold

in its
swift tissues, those

blown
ex-

panses,
shadows as

if
pouring, light

from your
fingers, your

blue, un-
loosened sash.

AND THUS UNTO

"... that the earth might be made sensible of
her inhuman taste . . ." —Djuna Barnes

"ne la perds pas"

1

flares chestnut, in
deep gusts
of wind . . . . is *their* world, Saint
Sulpice, the
whispers,

clicking dice-
like, mix

with our voices, rotate
through
the milky
astringent jade . . . .

~

that even the
bones, our

least breath be
swept
into those speculated wastes . . . .
(way that, spread-
winged, the

puffed marble, the
stars
at the tip
of their stiff petals flutter,
hesitate).

~

as if . . .
as if, in
that breaking, the
vocable

would open,
ave-
vacuous of the eternally deferred.

in jars the
creams, thin disks the
rouge, rubbed in
taut ovals
over the flush of your cheeks.

2

Paris
arboreal, its
bough
of dense mirrors
blown into branches, invisible
beaks.

are as
if gathered,
lifted . . . . the
limbs

as they
grapple: point.

what pigments, the
flared bells
of whose robes would float —whipped
gold— across
all that
abandoned decor?

~

Sèvres-
Babylone; in
updrafts,
off

your
tall forehead, your
soft horns

scroll. to
speak
of that stillness; to see you, and

still speak.

~

worlds un-
ravel
worlds, the

wrought heavens: our blanched
reflectives.
would
leave, who'd

perched, already, a tribe-in-
flight, at the
breath's

flaked
edges.

~

weight-
less, that
gaze, a

gray fume, chaliced
in ivory . . . .

                    that the brush
catch
on its fires; that the night climb,
light, a light-
articulate, off our tapered fates.

FLOWERING ALMONDS: OUTSIDE AND IN

it's a heart   that's
staring into the   damp petals; the   eyes

understand this.

---

washed altars of
white   coral, that depth-   ascendent . . .

---

the weight-
less tracery of the   lost face, ever-

a- metaphor-   away.

---

that the flowers aren't   ours, aren't
flowering for our   voices, but

the dolorous air's, their white   deliveries.

---

of shadows, the
first: cast, like

foam, across the   furrowed earth . . . .

---

wild buds on their wind-
ballasted antlers, beast struck,
its love belling dumbly in the rain-
darkened rose.

---

brought the sprigs in, the
blossoms, the rooted pearls of the
dew, everything
but the bees.

---

that we outlive this sweet
archaic spring, feed on
its slender wood, with
no measures but our own abandon.

---

a bowl of flowers . . .
a face
in the palm of its gaze: these, *these*
only, windows
opened wide.

BREATHHERD

1

. . . blown snows
lacing the
high precipices, Robion
ocherous, beneath, I
blew the

lamb-
transparent, in
loose

ripples, before me . . . .

~

flared
ground, fanned
thrush, in shadows the
treasured
ice.

were tethered
inseparable, wed for-
ever to these
bone-

less
drafts: the
driven interval's.
breath-

herded up-
wards, onto the
worn, wind-
riddled ledges, your

bells
beat silent

off my vaporous horn.

2

nothing that
was
wasn't twice . . . .

wandered,
charred
white, over the
spine-

eyed thistles, to
tell you, my tousled
angel, *holly,*
ivy,
acorn,

words
that you'd never hear.

~

a last
village spread, in a
fresco of
glazed angles, before
us . . . .

geese
jeered at the
moon's

wizened crib.

you were, and
weren't.
were the heavy tuft of
my darkness, come
un-
done . . . .

                    cracked
walls, coarse sheets!
in

that tall
glacial room, to
lay my-
self down, the length of
those

cold oils, quick
fleece, the
breath

reach rooted

into
the radiance it breathes.

CARDPLAYERS, CAVAILLON

for tiny
sums, the

hearts
slip . . .

(smooth

knuckles,
erratic

thumbs . . .)

. . . each
hand

narrowing,
fans

out, folds
back, deals

its
oblivious

fates . . .

---

by lamp-
light, a

crack
of fresh

cards,
rush

of sleeves,
like

censers
the

black
ash-

trays
fuming . . .

---

slim
mirrors the

thumbs,
rubbing,

wedge open.

---

mock-

recoveries
of an un-

sound-
able loss,
that

trim
flourish,
mne-

monic . . .

---

squints
wet,

porcine, his
lip-

tethered
smoke

coiling, *bleu*
céleste.

---

or, in a
ray

of hawked
gold, a

wrist

spinning
kings.

---

pe-
nultimate

nurseries
of

night, a
breath

held a-
beyant

in
a draft

of plied
numbers . . .

---

wizened,
a

nodding
odd-

man-
out, nick-

named
‘the

numb
angel’

---

as
these

sleights-
of-
life,
pinched

into
tiny fans,

spread

scarlet.

ELEVEN QUATRAINS AND A NOTE FROM VENTADOUR

for Brad

neither this world's, nor
another's, that broken house with
its books and wind,

bells sewn on the breathing veils, between.

---

with their wire, moon-
flat baskets, came searching
for the rain's meat, those
readers of ditches, dark margins.

---

as if listening, in
that barge of
blue chalk and choked linen, to
her own waves as they rose . . . .

---

over the fixed smoke
of the almonds, the other, the
gypsies' (their rabbits roasting

in the wind-
less light . . . .).

---

untouched, grown monstrous
with my own shadows, o
hooded lilies (the
suns shimmying upon the skin of the ditch).

---

way the eyes slide, an
instant slower than the face, the
hair lugged —like a trophy— over
the shoulders, after.

---

you only could
take your gaze from my keeping (tease it:
cold, nebulous, through
the taut shadows of your teeth).

---

the heart forever offered, en-
trusted to its own
perditions: that weird inadmissible rose,
valentin froissé.

---

glances, back-
wards, through the vaulted loop
of her arms. rasp,

as the blue rhinestone hairclips
slip under.

---

in these white shadows, the wind-
light we live in, would perish
without the word-
pleated waves: that
cadence we give them.

---

as the petals catch
against the blond canebreaks: say,
say nothing; it's enough, if

a wrist went blind on its own whispers.

---

always towards the end, the
grammarians. *albas*, our
dawn songs: on what terraces,
onto the carved waters
of what viol
shall our hearts be pitched?

GIRANDOLE

1

towards dawn, the
taxis
        idle
before the glass doors . . .
. . . .
fuchsia,

where a blown hem flares
in the sudden
updraft,
then

settles
pearl, through
a broken
foam

of reflections.

~

an ankle
arches, as the
mouths open, and fill . . .
a world-

without.
what the instinct
would swell to: that

image, that
deep

ray-
headed mirror
in which the dark breath
un-

wrinkles.

. . . .

wrapt
shadows, swept
fates . . .

                    in the rush,
uptown, the
moon
slips, over and
over, off the polished
wings

of the streaked
fenders.

2

it's how the
scarf falls, and
the

soft
braided silver
of the shoes . . . their signs!
that sky! the
new

un-
declinated night!
whisper

chases whisper, edge
its edges,
as

an arm swims
toward the
cast
brass palmleaves
of the light.

~

break, but
where; shatter, a
wave, still
swelling, against what? . . .
. . . .

. . . no
heaven, and
scarce-

ly an
earth, a-
wash in that last echo: a
mouth, as it

twists
to the fold of a shoulder.

II

Carnets

1979

for T. F.

. . . air
scarcer, fed
on the tooth's

twisted
shells (is *in-*
side it

begins: even
those long
lunar

plains we'd
crossed
on, the black

frozen dugs
of their
almonds: were

things the
breath
first fluted:

expelled . . .).

---

for the words fill, swell to their sounds, but only at the propitious distance.

our breath: reflected past us.

---

wanted the
wave   the lip-
curling sea-

verb, ledge of
the

hesitant
in its throe

forwards . . .

(near Maussane)

where the
boulders rose
on black
rafted branches.

---

was (you called it) the
tease of
life, what life   left out that's
luring it   onward

. . . still the
images to
feed on, crouch
to (that crumpled

gold).

---

even to
touch one
an-

other, a kind
of
telling . . .

---

all air swells into such tiny wrinkles.

(lightning's roses).

---

turned in the
tall mirrors, face
caked white.

---

was winter, when the doors burn like bright organs.

wherever: was for taking my shadows to.

driving them into the very midst of those wild reflections.

(voice-seeds, teased to the lips).

'On se perd à jamais, à partir de l'instant où quelque chose se passe. Tout est là, hors de nous.'

an eye afloat over a shoulder (Piero).

a hand hanging limp, luxurious, over its scarlet shell.

fed on those moments, as from a dark bowl.

their mock, momentary burials.

where, at world's end, had seen the small winds breed . . . .

and the hunched ivory of the irises.

(writing: was what there was).

---

as the
thirst that needles the
current, hurls
its
flat pearls
backward.

1980

(le jour de l'an)

snow in
the hills, the
roses opened in candlelight.

---

were like weights moving in a full wind: erratic, sumptuous.

thrust forever towards that instant that would take us.

(towards —certainly— some greater loss).

spoke, that the air stare backwards.

(there, where the syllables, reaching past us, would pile: cluster).

altars, our deep aggregates.

stars burning from the tips of the charred poles.

---

floated, sonorous,
from its tattered ends, my knot-
transparent.

---

in a script of
rock, would
have lain
myself in-
to your lightness,
ash (is
what's *between*
that

bears us).

---

shoved up, like
    two waves wedged,
hung

there.

---

eyes gazing into what the breath would eviscerate.

the bodies as obliterators: for grinding their shadows in.

blown marrow: our tokened hollows.

as we moved through the very mirrors we'd cast.

(those successive, archaic betrayals).

---

breath-
thin, the creams,
that
ex

quisite mask . . .

---

would travel the length of some taut, indissoluble rhythm.

naming, as we went, only the illegible.

(the white deck of its whispers).

temps lisse: that drift.

through the very midst of the eliminated, in the wake of that ragged wing-beat.

(the banished angel's).

---

hysteria's
mirror, our knuckle-
star in *penumbra, umbra,* a whole
ocean's shadow, on

edge.

---

there should be words for saying so little.

music, as it moves, ever a breath short of its reefs.

1981

in
tatters, time's
end, the

long threads
drift   gilded . . .

---

as ponderously, the bodies rise, pull free.

drawn into the tow of their dark, cellular mirrors.

fallacious, celestial.

(as if time itself had perched in its *bibelot* of worn, ivory branches).

as if world, at last, were letting us out.

. . . held
only

here, in
these
sudden

ver-
tebrae
of

breath . . .

this
word, my
name, your
voice

as you
name
me, my
one

in-
stance.

---

knew you by the elisions: that deep, inconsolable drift.

as if zodiacal: that transit.

elusive, those worlds with their watery fabrics and bright, weightless accessories.

the thick-lidded jars of their solvents.

(as if even grief were a pose struck, a glance held against so much dispersion).

---

burst as they
surface, the soda's
black
seeds.

---

a fate's for flying to.

sheathed air!

to the very tips of the lashes, teased.

---

who'd
twisted the

stars
thought-
lessly, looped
them

through that
rope
of

blown emerald . . .

---

as a gaze slid, flaking, from a shoulder.

down, through the stress of an instep, to that serried toe.

---

panic, the
void's

elected pearl, skipping
upon an
un-

numbered wheel . . . .

---

was what the words would rush to.

would fill.

like waves, chasing the scooped and wobbling heart of their own craters.

like a mumble, as it kneels to a null.

---

down wet
Seventh in
an un-

gathering
turban

of
exhaust . . . .

---

space, as it opens, ever in default of a face.

(deaf lilies; shattered calendars).

---

stood, limbal,
a-

mongst
the
bright updrafts,
an

up-

draft,
my-

self . . .

---

to the earth's very edges, where the words would turn into mouths.

and the hearts, finally, fly.

1982

since all journeys taken
are towards those yet-
unwrestled images . . . .

---

for to say is to separate: set lust to number.

out from the mute-immediate (our ever-dismembering 'here').

to sprout, as signs, from their mirror-seeds.

(belonging, at least, to that: that errancy, its aisled measures).

as we lifted rocks from our eyes; lay them, akimbo, in our bleached meadows.

(tin roses, trussed idols).

while inventing memory as we went . . . .

---

where the seed-
beaded tops of the
grasses shuttle, went under (
were jars: what the long bodies
had hollowed: the dark milk
of these whispers).

---

where a breeze, all summer, was tugging at sound.

to do without us was what it meant.

because, as you'd approached the name, you'd begun losing your own.

as the self touches itself in its 'second person.'

the two masks: clattering.

---

un-
wrinkles, as the
heart would (were the
heart to

rise, re-
leasing, on
its teased streamers,
that taut, ir-

recusable motto
of

its own
un-

telling).

---

intricate maquillage of the imaginary.

(the pale traffic of its crystals).

who'd breathed these things into me, then drawn them —rhythmically—
out.

---

as the shadows
un-
muscle, and their   flashed milk
chills.

---

from the very tips of the pulled scarves: depletes.

(who'd stay; who'd thrive in the deep facets of some sudden, irretractable decor).

oak, then juniper.

the stars moving, as if sideways.

with nothing but 'interval,' its word, as talisman.

as what was given to answer ourselves with.

whereby things might be seen *in another light.*

---

not ourselves that translate, but
our works: star-   hoop of
sounds, our dark

stays.

---

being carried, by an excess, toward those first simplicities.

rhythm, the image-bearer.

where the poem would finally be seen as the running of its own unrelapsing interval.

as a sectioned wave: thrust forwards and, forever, reflecting back.

(lathed winds, siphoned honey).

creating, out of its syllables, that witnessing space.

like washed rings of invisible coral: those second circumferences.

at the very edge: the effigy.

where smoke would rush —vanishing— into its rolled conch.

and sound, at last, be received.

for the idol remains idol: is the inexhaustible coursing of its own inscribed rhythms.

---

even 'shatter'
as it

enters (pulsed
air of
those

heavens, our
breath-

heaps . . . .).

III

The Wizened Shrine

RAY

1

ploughed
ice, where an
eye

swims, scarce
muscle, up
over

its
clotted ditch
(*mine,*

is mine,
would
keep saying),

ray, swung
pendulous,
through

the rusting
wind-
knotted shoots.

~

just there,
where
the instant

wobbles, bowl
the
bluejay

rims, with a
jagged
beat shatters.

~

wrinkled, the
long
rocks, the

des-
olate scales
of the

oak. unto
what, journey
where, the

wind's nerve,
light's
white

tendril
on its
hooded stave.

2

would
enter. close
on the frozen

roses of
the cabbage,
the

light, at
last, *within.*
o world

where the
world
went, the slack

caves
of the air a-
gape, is

a shawl
of
burnt

crystals, spent
echoes
that's

falling
out, on-
to the lidless.

3

thread, the
sequence,
ray

welded —short
wire— to
the

washed
black
fans of the

cypress (*mine,*
is mine,
would say, a

squint leashed
to its
cold fires).

~

gather
branches, bear
stones,

bulbs,
fleece . . . . .
that they

be brought,
set,
vibrant, in

sound; that
light,
unto light's

last artifice,
be folded,
its

facets wrapped
within the
word's

cupped
shadow, and
wizened shrine.

IRISES

for Susanna

out of those wild, in-
visible circuits, a
hawkmoth flew in. was dawn (in
deep vases, the first
white lines of the iris).

---

way that they ruffle in
that rock windcell (that their buds un-
scroll and open: opened,

asking myself only for what I see . . . .).

---

like birds trapped in
those tall, still-
glistening frescoes: the errant etruscan's.

---

earth it-
self held
in

that silent
ven-
triloquy.

---

muscled in
washed golds or
waves   of pale naples, these deep
androgynies: a

joust of buds and   limp
relenting petals.

---

my lines, for an instant, become   theirs (but
only
for the   extravagation).

---

rise, loop-winged, in a   volley
of light yellows, stalks   caught
in slender   rectangular jars . . . .

---

being invisible, we
sip at those   open
emanations: tubers shot into   tall
grottoes, emptied
wind-   eaten tombs.

---

lovely, the irises in their deep
oblivion, wounds   open on
what the poem would
close: catch   in the purities of its fiction.

---

a surf of
frozen whites, for your eyelids; its
waves, that
pitched linen, for your sleep . . .

(faïence de moustiers)

not the javelins stabbing
into their own azurous mass, but the bowl, the
cold, sun- broken round . . .

---

are corpses, too: the petals streaming
against the hard stalks, or
wizened, sack-
like, in the tissued shadows of their wings.

(Saint Vincent's)

those cold fires on
their piped stems don't flower, they
alight, perch there in pale,
insane violets . . .

(are prayers, are the smoke of prayers . . .).

---

are awe-

weights (for
weighing

a

grief
against . . .).

---

the dead go on drinking, speckle
the white table saffron
with their transparent inks . . . .

---

each iris: the shell
of an iris, the papery craters
of its spent
ebullience.

---

mass gutted for the sake of an inference.

---

are the lines of flight of
these floral chases (not the
blades, the buds, the skirts blown, buff-
white, over the draft of
their thighs),

but the lines driven, quilled,
into the drawn lips of the invisible.

(viaticum)

the dried irises in the
sleeves of the   oil lamps
are yours —for   your journey— for dimming
those   gaudy winds with . . . .

LES ALPILLES: A LETTER FOR J.

wrapt to the
eyes in
loose, blue hooding, lugged —over the
last rocks— those
threaded
whispers. *Col*
de Vallongue, where the crows
unhook, and the
suns
rise, disheveled, with their winds . . .

would enter, had
said, slipping
light into
light, wedging dawn
   with those thin, splintered crystals.
in bowls,
the

glowing
crags. currents
that the goshawks, soon, would
take to.

ever the part, un-
worlded. at the errant center, that
locked muscle, the
mirror of
its

own unreflecting
integer . . . .

long straps, slapping,
way
that the path bobbed
against bone. that the scree jingled
with the spill of
its
black, ice-
lacquered blades.

La Caume, in
a drift
of barbed
thistles. *Glanum* greek, over *Saint
Rémy.* where,
once, the
stars got washed, the
cypresses still rose —swollen— into that in-
voluted
air.

higher, saw
the
Rhone dangle, and the
trembling tin
of

its spread
estuary. *Les
Baux* sudden, as if stranded, barge
floating fixed
over the
low, domed groves
of its olives. *Altas
ondas
que venez suz la mar,* sang Vaqueiras, who'd
worn the peacock, known
its pointed
star.

past *le mas de*
Chevrier, a
sputter
of flushed partridge. clouds rising, like
Elijah's, in high,
wind-
piled spirals.

winds;
would learn
the

winds' names; in
oc, the
words for 'moss' and 'mineral' and 'fern.'
for it's
through the words
we'd

enter, would
wed

that overhanging
jelly-
headed light. where path
would turn into pine, and pine into those
flaccid, ice-
green
fires . . . .

towards *le*
Planet
ruts run double, ruler-straight, across
rock. dwarf-
oak and
juniper —as conjugates— dropped
beneath the
last
aleppos, to *Saint*

Gabriel. the
plains, at

last, that pampered
ground. terns, working at the wheat's
edge; a canebreak,
a-

flame: smoke,
twisted
through brass. on the
tow-

path, now, towards
Tarascon,
ten steps, exactly, between the squat
platans,
pruned sheer.
the fields, now, as
they break
into gardens, and the ragged
quince-
hedges thicken. the bells, the
dense bells of *Sainte-Marthe* already, and the
black
workshops blue
with their heavy acetylene stars . . . .

would
enter, had said, the breath
sleeved, the
backpack jarring. over
and over, in a single, insistent murmur:
dwell, had said.
dwell, would
dwell.

CIRQUE: OR UPWARD GATHERED OUT

long
crossings, nights spent
in small, one-
star

hotels, o
breath-

dragging-
body: bore signs, ferns
for the

passage. for
feeding the
rocks

with. knees
tucked
under, on

those
currents, those
thin slips clambered, a
rope

shaking
shadows, an
earth

either side.

MANNA

for Gael Turnbull

all day, in the
    gorges, the sun fell
in pinched
showers,
pale

e-
longated sparks.
gathered

what I'd
found: the
gold-eyed sporangia: the
self-

combusting.
dust, the
dry

foam of some other, some
yet-un-
engendered world!
Miranda-

in-
rags, through her blue
cell,
mulling. sound
before

sense: molecular. that
it spill, in-
cipient,

from our
fingers, from the blade
of the

launched wave
break.

AS IT UNRAVELS

1

. . . . were
running through:
past one
an-

other (script-
less, the

ribbons; too
slow, our
taut

watery tapes . . .)

~

. . . . where
some-

times, a
wrist
would flicker, or
a
raised lid

wrinkle
gold . . . .
. . . . er-

ratic, that
data

of our continuous
dis-

persion, o
world,
worlds we'd
un-

ravelled
from our
hooded crypts . .)

2

where-
by, once, had

rooted . . . .
. . . .
. . . . stray
knuckles
sunk

in
dark oils, the
wasn't:
was; the
wind-, the moon-

strung
numbers spooled.
. . . .
(null's

pinched
hovel,
a-

round
which wrapt, and
gathered, and
grew . . . .)

~

grew rocks
and

meadows . . . . .
. . . . . grew the
shallow brass
of the

bells
for beating the
seasons
flat . . . .
. . . . . . sequence,

grew
sequence, those
sleek

channels we'd
travelled
on:

image
dis-
placing image,
the now-

insistent-
on-the-next, as
the

slipped air, a-
bout us,
un-

reeled . . . .

~

lighter, ever
looser,
the

new fabrics . . . .
. . . .
fainter,
in

their burnished
ovals, the
thigh-

piled
bacchants
float . . . .
. . . .

would
close, en-

close, worship at
our own
edges . . . .
. . . . ever

an-

other, another's,
a
mouth rises

as the wild eyes
change

color . . . .

3

breed demons,
breed

light . . . .
. . . . . . are held,
dis-

pelling,
emp-
tying earth
into

air . . . .
. . . .
. . . .
twist, out
of

quick syllables,
the
wings, the
wing-

beaten forms we'd
give
to the
in-

admissible . . . . .
. . . .
. . . . shape
the

vacant (where-
by
the words . . . . .
. . . . where-

by the
words would pre-
cede
us, would lay

our
own measures past

us . . . .)

~

. . . . past
the

last
voices, in a wreck
of

white
petals, the
air, the
air's, that our
own

resonance, at last,
receive us . . . . .

IV

The Earth as Air: An Ars Poetica

Tout le mystère est là: établir les identités
secrètes par un deux à deux qui ronge et use
les objets, au nom d'une centrale pureté.

Mallarmé

for Esther & Gabriel

I

1

lapping of light over
light, dew podding the tall
ferns nacreous, as
it
opens (that

~

even here, at
the very edges it
start up, this teasing of
sound out
of

substance: the
air
paired fibrous
with

syllables: *moss, rock, air-*
it-
self-in- syl-

lable, that
it

happen).

~

in twos, that
it ribbon forth, the
forked idiom's . . .

each thing
eithered to   another, the   *this*
whatevered to the
                    that, the
ark-

within-the-
lyre-   propellant: *wind*
and *white roses*

wrapt in a   taut, vibratory weave.

~

because poetry is passage. is an equipoise-in-motion, addressed *away.*

by juxtaposing syllable, word, word-cluster in a harmonious tension, the poem (both in its materials and its sonorities) channels that passage: determines its course.

(or atomically, by the poem's vibration; discursively, by its dialectic, its *tao).*

is the body's, first, its profound androgyny's.

fused, inarticulate: insufferable.

that the saying, in releasing, separates: investing each of its opposites, its multifarious twins, with a transparent identity.

that only as 'eviscerates' might they enter the relationship, the *passacaglia,* the poem.

as our breath's oscillating bodies . . . .

is *wind* that permits *white roses* (and inversely).

locked together in their lyric trajectories of attraction, contact, dispersal.

far, what the poem would gather, accord, scatter further.

the earth, in its longing, its shattered fragments —in twos— fluted through.

celebrants in the doom of their invisible transactions, the narrows of their weightless encounters.

that's neither the *enactment of* nor the *symbol for,* but the rites of process by which substance, through sound, is transmitted forth: towards . . . .

the lash-undulant of complements that's

2

neither the   lily's
nor

the toad's, shem's   nor shaun's, all
our adored decoys of
                    cognition . . .

(what language
had   seized, set
                    echoing, reflexive,
through the chambered
spaces
of
our words.

the bounced clowns of history, one
the suspended
referent
to the other: ever, our
alien- commensurates).

but,
what rushes
be-

tween them:
slips
be-

tween
cabbage
and

spade, thumb
and
clay, in

a gust-
accelerant
of

ashes,
shadows,
of 'things

that are
not.'
neither

earth's
nor
air's, but

the
null
springing,

ebullient,
out
of

a fusion
of
either's. the

nei-
ther's, the
limp,

re-
lapsing
flora of

their
muscles
dulled in

the
wisp, the
wires, the

un-
elemented
rays

shot
from the
hinged

half-
shells: the
echoing

limbs
of these
lovers.

~

that
it happen!
that the

breath
leap, and
the dark

light
issue, be-
tween

our tongue
and
teeth!

II

1

in taut banners of shadow, the scrolled motto of the vacuous, unravelling . . .

whipped, vibratory.

being nothing, in itself: an otherwise-isn't, except for the syllables, either side, that channel, sluice, project it forth . . .

there, just *there,* where the syllables touch, join, and in their lyric reverberations: *release.*

and, in so doing, radiate outwards themselves in a sonorous diffusion: an effluvium.

annulled, in successive pairs, by the impact, the discharge, of their matched percussions.

a 'nothing,' then, propelled by a 'neither.'

a conveyed omission.

the vector of a dark and running silence within the resonant catch-and-release of every poem.

wedged as we are, as our sounds are, into twos: supplicants, each time, to that current; that sudden, unsubstantiated breeze.

that soundless bolt in the unwrinkling tin of its quiver.

Being through being (no *Sein* without *seiendes),* as the shadows transit: slip from the intricate cage of their syllables.

radiance of 'sea: moon: pearls: tears,' its compressed immensity.

that it open, break: *irreflexive.*

light's for letting light out.

the poem: for the shelling, the pulping.

'everything I've created has been by *elimination*' (Mallarmé), 'and every acquired truth comes from the loss of an impression that, having glittered, faded, and, in the subsequent release of its shadows, allowed me to penetrate ever further . . .'

to work by elimination implies not a lessening, but a translation of intensities: an *othering.*

as we articulate *away* from ourselves in a continuous elision *towards.*

as the poem comes free of its speaker . . .

kept, as we are, from entering what we say, from pursuing what we imply, we create a space, each time, from which we're excluded.

the poem is, as such, a quit body: a quittance.

a locution-in-displacement, in ritual flight towards its own reception.

towards that ear, that ether, that *absentia* of all presence: presence itself.

alighting, touching, as it does, upon a separate exhilaration.

and carrying within it, as its null, its no-breath, perhaps the lightest and least palpable of all vapors: that of death itself.

but a death continuously discharged, expelled, projected . . .

a death *kept alive.*

driven from the hoard of our bodies, and cast: oscillated outwards by the syllables themselves: by the play of their tensions, the purity of their releases.

that together, they alight (the 'nothing' and its 'neither,' vector and effluvium) in a luminous tapestry of sound.

the power of its shadows caught —and thus neutralized— within that crossed, inclusive weave.

that depth-conciliative.

neither living nor dead, now, but extravagated, an *ex-vita,* and thriving, twiced, upon the profound surfaces of a second, an alternate space.

as it happens: as the lyric accedes.

through the wind's zero: penetrates.

as the word-errant —at last— touches upon the silence of the word-inceptive.

as if returned, restored to some verdurous, subliminal condition.

in a wash of leaves, waters, songbirds.

aside from the music, inaccessible.

as substance (converted into sound for its passage forth) reverts, at that given depth, to a *still matter:* to the quiescent music of its particles.

in a dimension that we've metrically fashioned, projected past us, and
assembled forever *to our own exclusion.*

that substance might transit through us.

unto that grace, that specific perdition, might be received, safeguarded,
preserved in its infinite distillations.

not as our echo or emanation or resonant gloriole, but as the exhumation
of the real, reintegrated.   as the essence of entity itself.

by which all things, unto themselves, are rendered.

by which, by uttering, we *are.*

2

not the
rose for its
damp

im-
pacted odors,
nor

tweezed,
semantic, to
a white

in-
cestuous eye:
our

im-
maculate
mirrors. but

the rose
as votive: for
the

vow
of the rose.
that

washed
in the
cold foam

of its
cratered
petals, is

offered,
boned to
an emp-

ty density
by our
breath.

~

o oceans,
in the
heaving

wilder-
ness
of the

un-
cradled
heart, that

the rose be
blown,
spewed,

beached in
the
trans-

parent
salvage of
its

round-
ed
syllable. that

it
weigh, at
last, *one*

with its
absence. as
the rose-

votive is
laid
on the

scalloped,
ray-
blazing

shrine
of the rose-
iconic,

and the two
roses, ac-
corded,

resound.

III

hég *wuḍ 'ámjeḍkam*
that-one is from-thing

it [spirit] is its [signal's] source

from *Piman Shamanism and Staying Sickness*

1

because to stay means to send.

means to maintain this tension, this exclusion, this *physis;* in residing, to defer.

sending, instead of ourselves, our syllables.

(the breath we'd drawn, still threaded, out of our buried mirrors).

gutted tokens, blown shells!

because it must be given: this space-unsustainable (is, perhaps, our one imperative).

its words, worked free (from where, still swelling, we'd break: feed crouching upon our shattered reflections).

but teased —diminishing— into immensity.

to a traced erasure.

to where, inverted, replicated, the two roses, in equivalence, would touch.

would twice.

the created, at last, syncretic with creation.

sound, sounded: plumbed, vibratile (shadow and syllable) unto those rippling, mineral tissues. that 'against-which,' reverberant.

that depth, auroral.

out of which, once, as 'from-things,' the words first devolved.

(while cryptic, within them, hid the roses, the oceans).

that earth be but the dark, sparkling residue of that blown emanation.

our presence *here* but the distance-from.

dense, lexical, deferential.

expelled, as we are, and possessing nothing, finally, but these words, rattles, wind instruments.

these relegating agents of the ruptured air.

for 'in huts, man dwells . . . endowed, godlike, with that most perilous of things: speech.'

that *here* exist, but in the tension; and *there,* in these released syllables posited, deferred.

in space, re-constellated.

over and over, instead of ourselves, *past* ourselves, as if sacrificial.

(the breath, scuttled; the voice, boned).

2

by which each
thing, unto its sign-
auspicious, is
rendered:

reeds,
rockfish
and crystals, the

brief
calices of
the winds-
in-

flower . . .
(were each
things we'd

seized,
tempered,
held ballasted in
the pressed metal

of
our words (while
their shadows thickened
off
our breath's

slipped bells).

~

but thinned;
blown, in-

candescent (to where
the words, in
reverting,

would flare . . . .).

by which
wheat
and gypsum,
lightning and
shell . . .

by which
marl,
starling, and
elm.

~

because, if we
stop, stop hollowing
substance, and ex-
tracting sound,

stop feeding the
stars
with
their barbed
syllables, then the
stars, certainly,

shall
have us . . .

for
certainly, there's anger
in the un-
named: in roots and
pebbles, in   the limp
rags
of   the running air . . .

is, in each
word, un-
rendered, the noxious light
of its   hoarded
shadows.

(for never
had the heart moved
through
such wilderness; never
in holding, had
we

held less).

~

that the
either,
finally, open   and
the diptych, in
its creased whispers,   spread . . .

for the sign:
the
sign's trans-
parent. the

earth-worded's a
station
in
space!

tide-keeps,
wind-
keeps, we
stay, that
each thing, in
its magnitude, be
inserted;
in conjunction,
set.

that,
through us, the
hazel
might ripen, and the stars
into their
fall quadrants
drift.

that, word-

herded, the
rocks, orchards, and
waves, the

feathered
whales, unto
their twicing, be

acquitted . . . .

~

        sorrow, too,
                that in sending we
stay; that   all else transits
                ex-
                cept ourselves.

        are that it   be.
        are that it   thrive: the
sun, in its

        washed
        fires, sal-
        vaged;

        each thing,
        in
        its buoyed scales,
                as-

                signed.

                ‘in huts’ to
        witness,
        restitute   what is . . . .

        unto
which, as
        offering, this   discourse
                                        would rise.

Voyaging Portraits

for René Char

I

Of Neither Wind
Nor Anemones

OF NEITHER WIND NOR ANEMONES

opening, one
after another, our
last definitions (way
that the rooms grow, the wrist feeding
on its own words: dark foam,
'inexhaustible flower').

---

the tips of the self fill: suffuse, but
only towards
extinction (what the
wrapt mirrors, in their passages, extract).

---

otherwise, of those opaque bodies in
their moving fields: no
word.   is only the glint that utters (or

promises to).

---

you far, even further now
in these vacant
creations.   through the
summer's smudged transparency, not even
a teased shadow, slick,
across a quivering lid. . . .

---

thrown over and
over onto that hollow heap, the heart
makes its answers (but
only as it falls, only

as something light, wasted as itself
reverberates).

---

would wear that cloth, that
exhaustion (the spent
head of the crystals embedded: en-
shrined), o bodies beating
against their own translucence.

ALONG LINES THE LINES MOVE

along lines, the
lines
        move (so damp, all
spring, the
sweetpeas rose, as if
sipped —pink, carbuncular— into
ilex

and pine.   festooned,
im-

possible!).   along
lines, the
pressured fragments: steel, ‘nacre,’
dew. . .   the scrapped
world’s: was
what

we’d drawn, quickened
into taut, running strips
of
sequence.

                                shale fitted,
intricate, to
foam.   breath-set, the
sectioned waves (were what, in
saying, would take
us.   a-

long lines, the
lines: is how the
wrist

works, and the linked, articulating
bones of
the

light.   is what
would bring
us: of

all words: 'you,' the
furthest;
            would bring
our arms
under, a tongue

twisted
through teeth).

                                        . . . is why the
grapes loom, and the
crinkled
hearts

of the hollyhock.   a bulge
of ocher
over the black
abutments.   way, ways: in
a

flush of wind, your
tall body
flares
into focus.

IDYLL

where the pine-
needles bristle, like
blue
sequins, the

mirrors
burn.   so

many knuckles
for that
hand-

ful of
words: path
springing —mineral—
out

of path.   wind I
drop
through, sleep in, a
lobe wrapt
in

the plump
muscles of a mouth. . . .

~

knead and
grapple.   bury us in
that

breathing.   for
earth's

its own
twin.   that
pressed, the

bodies im-
print.   print canyons,
thistles.   rise,
wet-

flanked,
from the driven image
of our

own ir-
retrievable limbs.

NILE

for Jolaine

of wheat, of its
crisp
metallic ears,
the
deep

shuttle
of its blond stalks
seething: these,
of
these, of

what-
ever the breath
would bundle, barge
of

moons, of
moons, too, the
fresh-

ly
enveloped . . . . . .

~

as if
lidded, that

light, that loosened
hair, gone

under . . . .
. . . .
hauled
world, 'beginning
in

inventory,
census, writ.'   was
what
we'd

brought: a dark foam
breaking, circle-
upon-

circle, haunch
and
flower, re-
verberant, with-
in
those

crouched
encompassing domes . . .

~

like
touch itself, then,
that
sudden

reception, that
salvage, those
slim

bells, stranded. . . . .
. . . .
. . . . ('for-
ever,' had written,
'had
journeyed
for-

ever to
edge space, to bring

our images
under. . . .'). blown
tokens, scooped
shadows, the
idea

of arch, ogive and
shell. that the
breath, at

last, be imprinted;
that the hearts,
those half-

mirrors,
fold . . . .
. . . . down

through the
flayed air, tongue,

wrist,
ankle, foot: that
lowered

gold.

~

of you as
form,
as

volute, as where
my least words ride:
pile, rhythmic.
(where

each whisper
would accrete, o
glut
of crystals, the
deep-

ly inscribed . . . . . .)
. . . .
is where, at
last, *was, am, would.*
utter,
the

breath as
it

breaks (where the
wind,
squinting, had eyed
its

entry) . . . .
. . . .
. . . . . . o grottoes,
polyps, bright

cages
of light: those

worlds-
with-

in, in
which nothing's,
finally, further. . . .

WHAT THE MUSIC WANTS

in memory of George Oppen

what the music
wants is
pod and tentacle (the thing
wiggling,
wild

as washed
hair, spread).   is our-
selves, in-

serted.   within
our
own rhythms: wrapt, voluted,
that miracle
of
measure-

ascendant.   *to*
stand, that there's some-
where to

stand.   marble
over

moorings, the
scaffolds, now, as if
vanished, and the steps, the
floors: spoken
forth.   *to*
stand, stand there, with-

in
sound alone,
that

miracle!

                                        is what the
waters comb, and the
bells,
beating,
count (faint, now, over the

waves, in a
garland
of
bells).   *is*

somewhere, and
wrapt

in the bulb
of its
voices, are buoyant, among.

TRANSPARENT ITINERARIES: 1983

as the distance, its un-
flowering screen, drifted —a pure
interval— be-
fore us . . .

---

it's the inference, not the inferred, that draws, seduces, abducts.

. . . sleek panels of the labyrinthian . . .

as each thing discloses another in an uninterrupted game of spatial displacements.

the signs, billowing like sleeves.

who'd bring the body —fully focused— to its very tips: its burning termini.

(raw roses, slipped crystals).

between the pasted heart and the pasted image: 'obsession' as some belated form of measure.

that glint: its teased fires.

(as the eyes rise —wild— through their speckled mirrors).

---

had tested sounds against their own
transparence, shaped waves into
cast white claws (o world-

again-earlier, and ourselves within as
if swelling . . .).

---

weighed shadows against the back of our hands; hammered flames.

worked the red marigolds into long, faceted syllables.

writing: by which we'd create our own qualifiers.

---

amongst the
random, wind-
geared planets, their
idle

per-

egrinations, ours
as over-
sight, as
stella

syntactica.

---

goatbells moving on the far side of the dark bushes.

would rise early, take trains to the ruins.

(aloes, oleanders).

the images seen as offerings, as given (vowed) to the movement (the rhythms) that, in turn, would ravish and consume them.

---

pawned
our-
selves out, limb

after
limb.   in the
gray

caves of the
surf, where the
roses

get ground, the
breath
breaks

into petal. . . .

---

where everything would be perceived in pleats (wedged instants), or in the pleats' releasings.

. . . dense enough to lie the length of . . .

matter is what we'd ultimately extract from image, from idea (but a matter coded, ciphered, scored . . .).

awoke to those dim whistles: those slender, ash-blue birds, like Sassetta's.

where dawn still floated with its water-stars.

(who'd measure —as if one could— the immensity of this interruption).

o oaks, our first altars.

where only language, finally, the voice-wrapt-in-its ray, might intercede.

TRANSPARENT ITINERARIES: 1984

for Claude Royet-Journoud

grammar itself at
the very tip of each card, the
months rushed, slipped
under. . . . according to the predicate, would
grapple or stray, sip sometimes at one another's
reflections.

---

as if to match image with its ever-dissolving models.

(what fell, weightlessly as waves, through its own fires . . .).

as arbitrary, as determinant.

whole weeks spent —suspended— between one chord and the next
(Gesualdo).

took 'wind' out, took 'clouds.' left 'this' (was where we'd sleep).

---

a face, so sudden, moving
against no panel, accumulating
no appreciable depth.

---

or a wrist, twisting —in half-turns— through jade.

each feature, teased to a focus.

(breeze-needles).

as if what we'd fashioned, utterly infused, might —of itself— emit, radiate, *inform.*

---

tensest of
petals,
tasted one
an-

other in the
deep

crease of
those
screens. . . .

---

breath-struck, the arms, shoulders, sex: the guesses we'd made, the definitions we'd given ourselves.

draft-star, our speculated drift. . . .

would change stations, octaves, the whole scale of that sonorous ocean.

(were the lightmen, you wrote, who'd arrived first).

"tout était faux, absurde, épatant, délicieux," Matisse.

skidding tips of the breakers, those gates, entries, those long rooms we'd driven towards, all night. . . .

(piled hearts, that heaped linen).

where the gray eyes, gone under, emptied their image.

'like foam,' or later: 'like lost footage.'

no longer needed us, our spent pronouns, for pulling its moons through.

---

so much light, gone
un-
gathered: words
no one
would wear. . . .

---

where some sound (some labial) might have kept the cave open.

those blown, ocher-speckled planetaria.

(thin slips of the parallel).

as, through the otherwise unoscillating wastes, would quaver.

carried that image, that other, that crumpled gold like some pressed tissue,
meticulously tooled.

(some tiny, mummified gland).

'like fire, falling.'

where, to a low row of stars, the eyes shrank.

ODE: FOR THE BUDDING OF ISLANDS

as a
long wave shaking
its

metals free, went
under. . . .   those
rooms, that
rush of

muscles, slipping
be-

neath
shut lids.   is
swiftness we mean:
thread

we twist to, wrap
in, the least
ligament keyed
to its own
out-

running.   hissed
syl-

lables, our deep
ciphers: the
wedged

breath issues.   the
burst light
a-

lights, o
rain
of
fronds, islands,
phosphores . . . . .
. . . .
. . . . . . our hearts
shall

be planted.   shall
be
fixed: the still-
quivering flags of
our

forage . . . .
. . . . be-
fore the
tow
takes us, ankles
caught

in
its knotted linens,
shall be

turned in-
to meter, rung by
ripples, the
rich

red
corals of metaphor.

II

Against a Bleached Viridian

TWO PATHS

soulèu

path, my
needle, my os-
cillating

constant,
would take
what

you'd drawn,
driven
under, that

narrowest
of
noons, glint

that
dis-
closes the oval.

luno

or this, this
dice-
white

harle-
quin, as it
humps the

wind's
last ledges:
tell,

tell me to
the
light, mouth

that's
filling
with pebbles.

ESCARGOTS

for Harris

. . . move
with the humid moons, those horned
calligraphers (on the slick tin
of their own inscriptions
slip).

---

or rippling the wet length
of their chance mirrors, drain —contra-
puntal— their cell-
ulated twins.

---

spirits, too, these
pluvarians (of the lost questions, the
rolled black opals of
reply).

---

myopic grope of
their slow marauding muscles (the earth's
dim nimbi and concupiscent
mimes).

---

or, under the
freckled thighs of the thigh-
high iris, sip
gold (the scrolled
wet volutes of metaphor).

---

towards dawn, ride
back, slip under. of their now-
untraceable instinct: these erratic
metallic glyphs.

---

whom, paraphrased, would set (ir-
reflexive, now) to the
slow bars, muted bassoons, of the
'parallel.'

---

that it might, thus,
continue, but other: otherwise. in these oblique
passages —the coded amphibians'— be
secreted.

OUT OF THE IDENTICAL

a hand's
writing the
rocks. . . . is
waiting

for its
reflections to

catch:
quiver. weeks,
now, without,
had

hollowed volume,
gutted
mass, rolled
the

bone of a
breath
over the

wind-
pitted ridges.
(were
words

for these words,
were
voices . . .).
would pull, from
the

flowing
light, each
feature.   draw,
from its

tissues, that
tissue, that

smoke, with its
vaporous,
verb-

driven shimmers.

ELEVEN ROCK POEMS

for Emmanuel Muheim

sent myself the length
of my own metaphors (boxwood, then cistus, the
swallows going white in the high winds). a
body wrapt a-

bout the mirror of its breath, slept
nights in the shallow, black waves of the rocks.

---

where ice lacquered the
red arrows rose, a wrist hoisted
its ankles after. lapped muscles, the
limbs-chromatic, would
reach, touch, be drawn through the roots of
that reaching.

---

up, out of the last, lime-
stone cirque, on footpaths a half-
foot wide, looked down. saw my-
self, as if
dissolving —washed blue, the back
still bent— as I climbed.

---

the eyes rising through those random
stations, their
wedged breath- holds (as if
'something' drew, pulled, as if
a 'somewhere,' finally, were).

---

as much dust as snow, the
trail's driven into
those deep, mineral creases (had carried
shadows, the bundled sticks of their tinder. over
the soft, billowing shrouds, had beaten

breath, pulled light from the thin meats of
each murmur).

---

all space, as it muscles in sound (im-
mensity driven, com-
pressed into such quick passages . . .).

---

chord the body hauls a-
cross the washed minerals, sporadic blacks
of the stout ilex, saw the fixed intervals
moving (and 'the
harmonies' as they shattered, strayed, re-

grouped).

---

high, now, over the river, where
millgirls, once, set the long-   wicked snails
flaming downstream, the

path vanishes, breaks
into boxwood, cade.   (shall weigh shadows; where the   thin
winds shiver, read
their mineral   palm).

---

for that itinerant breath-   pilgrim, may
the rock be hollow, *be*
grotto; within it, may the
ashes of those last   opaque vocables a-
light.

---

loss, each time, descending, as the
rhythms catch
on the quick loops of re-
entry, and out, over the   shoulders, the
rocks sprout, rise, un-
fold.

---

had plumbed space, sideways.   blown,
through its god-
less body, these showers of thin, hissing
splinters.   (that the

emptiness be edged, wedged, that   pierced, it
spread open).

JANUARIUS

. . . low, now, over
rocks, the
sun's
loose muscles, its running
squid.   January's
driven: an un-

buried
mirror, into
these
thin, jingling thickets. . . .
is

this: this maze I
move through, telling
me to
my-
self (like so
many slipped beads, the
breath, its

trans-
parent accretions).   *ankles,*
shoulders,
teeth.   but
who,

whose, unto
what
raised ground, in the
name of

which shrubs uttered, vowed,
given?

would bring
the syllables
under. sink flame,
fleece, the wind, in
worked

circles of sound. slake
shadows, assuage
ground. determine the depths,
the syntactic
weights

of the
parallel.

~

. . . and thus,
through my own murmurs, my laid
stations, move
past

me. of oak
and aleppo, the

octaves. of juniper —its glazed
berries— the shattered
bells.

FRAGMENT: FROM A BLOSSOMING ALMOND

for Theo

where bees
shadow-
box with the wind-
shuttled buds,
the

image de-
taches, gets

sent . . . .
. . . .
. . . . . . wrought
tokens, our
breath-

studded screens . . .
shall
sleep in the lee of
that

tremor, move
to
the cold

shaken scale of its
petals.

TRANSPARENT ITINERARIES: 1985

sounds, but
past
us 'the
tablets'

---

all things —and endlessly— in parallel registers.

(la mise-en-abîme)

as mass moves sonorous through its syllabic tessitura.

each segment, rendered pulsate, serial.

(what kept us —othered— to the strict liquids of reflection).

to our running scripts, our loose fictions, given.

---

oceans up-
right   at right
angles (the
                 roar

scored   )

---

as a body as if transits with its breath.

(each of our bright, beaten contours).

evolving, as we did, into tighter and tighter units of dissolution.

white, impounding white.

returning —as if one could— forever elsewhere.

. . . thrashed
leaves, our
knees

tucked under.

—what sent, wreathed in static, its stray signals, backwards—

all its rolling foam, in slow fracture.

. . . our buried
weights, tiny
pictures, were
what
we'd drink from . . .

A FLORA BEGINNING WITH VINEYARDS

over the
rolled vineyards, lilacs
pinch light,
would

hold the
mornings swell, that
image, those

images strung, like
wire, and running singed
into hair, heat,
the white

rooms the
skull

keeps.   (keep,
keep us: we're letting
our-

selves out.   are
emp-
tying earth.   that, heavy

with members, with the
twined weight
the

breath tools, we'd
lay the
thin winds.   pull, over
our

shoulders, those
painted
caves.   herd *holly,*
larkspur, the dew
that,

bulbous,
shatters the black grain).

III

A Portrait of the Self as Instrument of Its Syllables

"*. . . parmi les matinaux,*" René Char

As when milk is bound by the juice of the fig, Empedocles

for Robert Duncan

A PORTRAIT OF THE SELF AS INSTRUMENT OF ITS SYLLABLES

1

. . . was dark,
finally, crossing the Crau, before the
first, blossoming almonds
caught in
the

head-
lights, flickering —pink—
from

under.   cupped
flame, that frozen
sequence.   (was what
I'd
hold to: the instant-looped, -bezelled,
-set, now,
in-

to sound.   the
narrow orchards, now, as
they isle, rise
the

pos-
sibility, at least, of
iso-

lates).

~

a hissing of
walls,
reeds, wind-
breaks: the running
conjugate

of the
un-
interrupted.

(was
what brought me, first, 'a bag, and
briefcase,' the
pos-

sibility, at
least, of stations, intervals, of some-
where where the numbers
might knot, and
the
taut, white boulders, in their

breath-
lines: eddy

. . . would lie there, the full length
of that
murmur. 'not stillness,' said, 'but the
movement traced, gathered. the
loose skirts of the
flame in-
folded. mint

and japonica, brought —quartz-
like— to
focus').

a *where*, where
by the fibers might
run —refluent— into hip,
ankle,
tongue.

2

within the
circle that, hand-
stamped, cancelled the square: *Lacoste,*
fief of

oak-
smoke and iris.   of
moons

and nettles.   of the black
wind-
pitted cells of
its ramparts (what the
southwinds scooped, and the long
mistrals chiseled).   there, concentric,
at its quarried
heart, where
the

cobbles
fork, and the
hollyhocks

stand sentinel,
went

under.   where the
lamp
might root, and
the

low
room glow —bright

as burst
straw— brought
the

broken
swarm of my
syllables, a pulse

beating
against a diaphragm
of

shadows; a
face as
if
poured (so

many
facets) into the
depth-

less mask of its
hands . . . .
. . . .

. . . . that it
take!   that sunken,
the

damp
vocable sprout: a
'here'
huddled a-

gainst the
where-

less workings of
a scuttled
earth.   bed,
bottles and chairs:
that

each thing, as it's
uttered,
out of
its

breath,
smoldering, bud!

~

but didn't; wouldn't.   for
ten years, the
rocks wandered.   wouldn't stop: the
shelled meadows, nor the

knuckled trunks of the
stump
sycamores.   drifted Pisces, and Equuleus.
unbound,
un-
threaded, from the
slender wefts
of syntax, floated Sagitta, ashen. . . .
slipped,

what
could trace the weight
of
its own

fingers, bring
the meager echo —its stray body's— to
bear.

for ten
years, reigned
nomen, preponderant.   wouldn't fit, lay
broken, the
phrase, in its meted
progressions.   split, severed, what the
verb had
woven (a wave

through its
slack waters
shot, by its troughed rhythms, driven . . .).
a-

drift, now, in so
many
spent components.   in
nomen, the *mundus*
nominalis, each thing, unto itself, in-
vested; each, its
sole
and inflexible referent.   'like

unto like,' the limbs
un-
mixed: that vision Empedoclean, the fusion
of the elements, under
strife, riven.

                    shadows lapping
against chalk, for
ten

years, the
breath went, dis-
membered.   erred bone, erred
measure.   through the *nomen* (in its cell-
ulated
wastes) the poem moved, dis-
assembled, un-
spoken.

3

. . . . . hung there, a
damp
bulb, a plump
fire, from
under-

neath the
tangled coils
of

her hair.   whorled
taut, each
brittle,
in-

flammated node,
to a
flushed bud, each

knot.   then slack,
re-

lapsing, again, a
loose
effusion, a
heat, run un-

dulant, through
its

rhythmic,
lymph-

rippled grain . . . .
. . . .

~

rung,
am
rung to that that
draws and
in-

volves me; pulls,
cen-
tripetal, from
shank and

tongue.   urges its
glowing,
un-
sustainable image
—its im-

print, in
me— through that
narrow draft,
tendon
of

my own
an-

nunciations.   brings,
thus, each
word to
resonance, each

breath to
reception.   leads
the
least in-

crement into
that
tissue, that
globed air, that be-

gets.

~

. . . brings,
brings, thus, the
poem
for-

wards (of which I
am mere-
ly its
in-

stance: pre-
fix for setting
sub-
stance to

syllable.   for
bringing the
un-
worked images: *damp*
bulb, plump

fire, for-
wards, into their
linked

and sonorous be-
trothals).

~

for the words
wed as
they weave . . .   lithe, the
morphemes
couple, as the self un-
selves, and sends
its eye moving, deft, through mineral; its
breath, meshed,
through

pine.   mixes
flame,

flour and water; eschews
stasis; abets
rhyme.   binds the
goat's
milk fast to the
fig's
thick juices.

'not stillness,' said, 'but
the movement traced, gathered.'   but
sphaïros, the
earth bound, taut, to
its paired
releases.

4

for M.R.

over Goult, where the
lavender foams, and lizards —through
the dry
thyme— sizzle,
read
rocks.   read

walls.   saw interstice, manifest.   followed
the low, over-
lapping play of the stones, their ad-
justed
intervals.   past
Les Maquignons, clustered
in its crumbling,
rust-
red ochers, entered
the

trellised air, the wind-
scored

orchards.' (not
cadence, had

said, the fixed
fall
of its
quartered staves, but the wire drawn, the
lines

run rhythmic to
the folds

of the broken ground, pliant to
the earth's
un-

dulant
lay).

                    not form, then, but
'form, as
extension of content.'   but *gestaltung,* each
wave in
its
throe: the
gaudy heave of its

count-
less facets, a
fresh annunciate.

~

                    nights, would
read, *quouro lis estello*
brihon forço.   with-
in the tall,
lime-

washed rooms of that abandoned, dry-
stone cocoonery, read
Blake, read
Char, my

first masters.   the
flames rose, in

fat
needles, through the lamps'
glass sleeves. . . . with the least
breeze, the
slack
shadows throbbed. read

Sappho and
Pindar, Anacreon

and Catullus. came
birds, came reeds. out of
Isaiah, sprang summer; Parmenides, night.
from Dante, that
ore, that
ben

intellecto, and Ibn'
Arabî, those
suspended,
reciprocal

stars. came
winds, salt, marrows . . . for the lines, as
they run —transparent— into
dawn, into

light, bring to
each substance its qualities, each
reflection its
light. proffer their mettle; both
temper and

refine. came, thus, the
rivers. came fish, and
the

rain-
shaken lilies.   from the T'ang, thus, the
moons, and the Sung,
mirrors.   from

Mallarmé that
rush

of crushed
shadow, and Shakespeare, that
pearl, its
black

sphericity.   came
thunder, came
tin.   from

Traherne the psalm, burnt
to a glass
whisper.   from Hopkins the
bow, and Wordsworth,
verdurous, the
quiver.

                    . . . for the lines, as
they come, now, un-
written, as they run —pellucid— into
world, infuse, in-
still.   the
syllables fill.   from

Williams, thus, so
many wind-
petaled wildflowers, while from Duncan:
air, that
ayre exultant, and
Oppen, unrelenting, that wheel-

maker's
flame.   from
the

linguists, now (Whorf, Sapir)
how the
least
shift in syntax, tense-
perception, would
re-

set the
heavens.   bring a boulder to

tremble in the wrapt
tissues of a
breath.   bring, would
bring us, un-

centered, now, onto those very
first
fields: those re-
leased phrases of dust
and dragonflies.   adjunctive, now, to
that

deeper space.   unto that
far

heart, a people, cre-
puscular, who
point.

5

(The Translation of the Waves)

for D.F.

that air not
end, nor
flame
gutter.   that earth not coil —ingested—
into those nounal
hoards, but
verb-

herded, be
given: offered forth.   wind unto
wind, foam
unto *foam,* be pitched, sonorous; through each
meted particle, trans-
mitted.

                                        (for certainly to
own is
to interrupt.   to stock, pile, separate matter
from its own in-
nate motion —its thrust,
unto— to truncate
and kill).

~

. . . was
what brought me, then, a blue
shadow moving a-
gainst the
glass-

headed light.   a mumble, across the
pruned,
luminous oblongs
of the terraced orchards.   up, over Venasque,
where asters float
to the

fields'
very edges, climbed.
lavender, olive, quince in

laddered
octaves, came at
last to those
waves in
the

rocks.   that
cave

where the waves
hung from
the

poem's
high scaffolds.   *eine*
Pracht —that splendor— *das Werk*
der Wogen.   where, all
morning, they'd
amassed, lay gathered towards their own
trans-

lation.   a-
beyant upon the
brief: *schlägt es:* the
sea, in
Hölderlin's poem, all

morning,
pendant.

                                        of the way, the
various ways (angles, torque, tensions) the
waves
might break —fan
against the coastline, foaming— Fédier
and

Beaufret, all
morning, tested
predicates.   Heidegger withdrawn, opaque (a
block of
dark crystal, its
rays

bent in
wards) e-

lucidated the
verb, alone: its clipped, arrested movement.
the back
of his hand
slapped, flatly,
at the dry shadows.

eine Pracht!   all
morning, that
splendor!
that

cave ('no,
certainly
not
Plato's') where the
waves, in
their

great
watery greenhouses, ac-
cumulated: a-
waited transition.   in their high, fluttering
aviaries, their
transit.

. . . as
if, in that
vocable, all Europe, all

air —that long morning— were held, suspended.
as if, finally, in the
blue, in-

voluted
wheel of
that

verb-
transfigurant (in *all*
verbs, *all* mornings, finally) the breath would
slip,
accelerating,

towards passage.
wave

unto *wave;* surf bursting
against *shore;* each thing, unto its deep,
im-
bedded mirrors, pro-
jected; unto the running

parallel —its
referent— deferred.
that

thus re-
turned: unto the inviolate, at last, re-
stored, each thing might, in
its turn,
re-

generate.   out of that
lost
language, that buried resonance, might bud:
spring fresh . . . that
two-

fold, the
earth be —by
breath alone— its
own

recourse.   both
store
and sow, receive and diffuse, articulate its
re-
ciprocal spaces.   that it break,
thus, from that
ul-

timate hypnosis: the ul-
timate Gorgon's
white
monodic gaze.   from its
gases, be

saved.   from that flash and its instantaneous
white fires: *salva, salva*
terram.   was
what the

waves sang.   sang *save, save.*   what the
bells, off the tops
of the
tall waves, beat, flung backwards in
hard tokens, fat
hammered
froth. . . .

~

what brought me, then,
over the low
ledges.   brought that I
bring: impelled that I urge, herd, drive the
words into
that

luminous salvage.   and stand, there, in those
linked shadows, thus
lit.

IV

Along America's Edges

NINE DRAFTS FROM AMERICA'S EDGES

an eye's scanning   no
given station (where an-
other eye might have halted,   welled
some slight hollow).   is still, this
film: is playing itself out, its each
part equal.

---

would stop in those
long galleries of   white, marble-
wet buddhas.   be lidded in
their mumbling somnolence.   under, pressed
under, body the   breadth of
their absolving petals.

(Nantasket)

there, where the waves slide, no thicker
than sheet glass stacked in   flat
dissolving piles, a first jellyfish
stamped water with   metaphor.

(was the earliest of births.   of form, its nascent
displacements).

---

draws us, whatever's
out there, insisting so   on
our brief releases.   a charged lacuna
(pulling us, our
thick syllables, into its pursed,
successive creases).

. . . were talking to   walls, rubbing profiles
off the glass surface
of memory.   the lakes, you'd said, were
immaculate.   there, like steps, the
tall sticks dropped,
scales of some last, still-   dissolving notation.

(Rochester)

night after rented night, the   meat-
pink neons, the humming
of their   near-
liquid signatures.   said 'ready, am ready,' as
the heart   tugged at its ribbons.   knotted
them taut.

---

were words, entire passages
we'd leave   ourselves for. . . .   'barge,' its
bowsprit of
shadows, that the deep vessel be brought: flame
to an ir-
revertible focus.

(Waverly Place)

because the wind, there, is
the ocean's
fragments.   from cages, the   fierce
wells of   structure, pulled hair, fingers.   whipped
image (the glassy heart's) to a thin
consistent pigment.

(La Guardia, or the Flying Machine)

whereby, writing this, would
set myself to the   otherwise-
unremittingly-turbulent.   silver
through smoke, would ride to the   slip,
elliptic of
its diminishing metaphor.

VIOLET CITY: ASPECTS OF THE TRANSITIVE

saw the glass towers
slip,
        liquid, through the louvered
venetians; the light, in thin
strips, quiver
shut.
. . . .
call: call shapes, faces. . . .   each
'heart'
has its
number (its specific
fo-

liations).   even
here, as your

room
rises blanched, amnestic, an
        island, already, in its piled,
pulsate florescence: speak,
ring shimmers.   from
your

sibilants, shake
mass.

~

. . . falls, you'd
say, of
itself,
that
virtue,

breath-
tipped, that unbundled
fire . . .
. . . .

here, even
here, contours
table, chairs; runs —in pinched
ripples— to the linen's
slack
re-

lapsing
edges. (even
here —at this
distance, these late
stations— that script-vestigial . . .).

~

vine, out of
what
voices? fumes, buds, annunciates of
what
dead injunction?

puzzles your
wrist, now, the
tips
of your fingers. . . . you,
in whom its movement, moment-
arily, courses: its channeled
pro-
traction . . .
. . . .

would bring, to the
dark
mouth, its dark
syllables.   being
transitive, 'take, as object,' its
least creases.   into that
re-

cessive, still-indeterminate
image, the fixed
interval's,
enter.

~

. . . .
. . . floated bronze, once, in your
spread
fingers.   fanned damp,
expansive, a ponderous sponge,
in a
dull

shudder of reflections.

(the projected, at
last, depleted; the image
brought, taut, to that
burning con-
vergence).

~

. . . speak, even
here.   ring
voices.   for the word's
ad-

dressed: a flame
trained to its trellis.   from your
tongue,
now, tease
ash. . . .   here, even

here, in this
city

of surfaces (Manhattan, gone
violet, glossy, now, in its watery
up-
rights), ex-
tract measure, elicit
sound.

                    '. . . fumes, buds,' but
out of
what
scuttled work?   on which
extinct frequencies, those psalms?
a
breath's

lapping breath, limbs
limbs, that
that ray
shot, into its dark alveole, quaver.

ONLY IN THE MILKIEST EMULSIONS

(Beverly Hills, 1944)

only in the
milkiest
emulsions, the deepest
silvers, would
that

mirror open, the
tips

of the elbows
flare.   combs, lotions. . .
her sleeves
would

float over the
foam-
white bowls with their
na-

creous blossoms.   hair
shaken, hands
posed, each
glint a

splinter, a ray I'd
pull from
those

gray, grain-
in-

flected spaces. . . .
warped
oceans, our
ob-
fuscated worlds.   would
feed on

those fires, that light
that

pours in a
limp
clatter of black,
unfastened corals. . . .

ROAD, ROADSIDES, AND THE DISPARATE FRAMES OF SEQUENCE

W.W.'s

the road, that narrow fiber of running sounds, on which ineluctably—
you'd unravel.

both phrase and paraphrase of your own unbecoming.

(dropped gears; raised ground).

after the cholla and mesquite, the ragged dark triangles of the piñon.

—were as if fed to those spaces—

to the light's high, dustless, near-lunar intensity.

each pebble, as if pedestaled black.

each object, as if struck, petrified, held —in raised relief— by *fiat* of some
obscure, and now extinct, divinity.

travelled across, a 'transparent slide.'

as if to catch, unawares, your scattered, semi-conscious projections.

(that dim, disarticulated ore).

"Los Lunas"

—where a water tower, on its tall stilts, quivered silver—

(brief stations of the syllable).

while moving, now, as if past yourself, drawn into ever-increasing degrees of displacement.

so many voices, as if thinned, rimmed in static.

edged, inaudible.

(where, through the light chaparral, saw —staring backwards— a pair of hunched, high-shouldered coyotes).

—quills, beer-caps, obsidian—

the very instant the sun, in its ganglion of pink squibbles, went under.

the road, you wrote, began anywhere.

began wherever the words, out of the broken word, first rushed, irrepressible.

. . . the running tape of this sequence.

(wherever you'd finally rid yourself of any notion of return, of personal circuitry).

nights, even faster.

where the whipped ellipsis of lane-markers spun under, and past.

changed altitudes, frequencies, continuously.

(faint, now, the hiss and clipped, metallic snap of *maracas*).

near Albuquerque, neons, printing out palms.

saw (in an all-night diner) your own reflections as if splinter against steel, mirror, tile; burst —radial— to a thin, featureless spray.

as if, even thinner, only the words (the fitted whispers) might withstand fracture.

might wedge —like headlights— a passage.

(creosote in sudden frames through the black, glass-smooth curves).

—might, in some eventual reassemblage, reconstitute image—

what —nebulized— you carried wherever.

night after identical night, through those pink, cellulated rooms, that the mumble might persist.

its tiny, breath-bitten messages be sent, projected past.

(recorded, now, as if forwards).

as a dream breaks into its most indissoluble salts.

there, where one by one, cardinal then quail, the still-dark desert awakens.

(already violet, the mocha adobe).

'as a moon seen through the sockets of a puma's skull.'

were journeying, now, invisible to yourself; as if fictive to any eventual other.

—outcrops of red, sun-shredded rocks—

while far out, over them, the quivering mineral of the earliest mesas.

everything was there, you'd written, except yourself.

dredged air for that vanished anatomy.

(for whatever —once— underwrote 'lymph' and 'gland,' the 'paired heart of the indivisible').

clouds in thin, driven bands of crumbling nacre.

and, just beyond, on a last, laminal flake of scored sandstone: Acoma.

(a blush of smoke over its domed ovens).

'eye-dazzler' is the pattern, you're told, on those shattered fragments.

Haako, where resonance, first, determined habitat.

where voice and echo (off its sheer, vertical rock-face) registered identical.

—the chord, at last, accorded—

of the projections you'd send endlessly past yourself into the endlessly emanative: *that transcript.*

(the breath as if gelled in a bell of light).

five hours, now, of penetrated vacancy.   scattered *arroyos.*

now, only so many prepositions with which to fix immensity; determine, momentarily, a *locus*, an imputable name.

theirs, the 'directional shrines.'

there, where the gold poppies still wind-stiffened in the high chaparral.

breath-tooled, those spaces.

from Blanco's on outwards, a taut washboard, a wobbling, dirt ribbon.

(throb of your blue, wind-shaken sleeves).

'*there,* everything's *there.*'

would press yourself, full length, against the vertical plate of your own projections.   draw from its deep volutes.

(from each of its gradually unghosted vocables).

as if authenticating, as artifacts, presence and gesture; the very least ligament, rolled translucent.

Chetro Ketl.

where whole structures, once, were laid out, sidereal.

(a whole world, deferred).

followed, along the facing ledges, that erratic line of calendrical uprights.

'sun stones,' those squat, chalked-off boulders.

(you between, among them: at the errant center of so much conjecture).

pecked steps.

and —as if lacquered black— a high, cloudless sky, overhead.

towards Pueblo Wijiji, intense thirst.

would have drunk, if you could, from your lens' dark, watery reflections.

(where an eye —scarcely yours— floated over).

charred hearths.

and a random marker, occasionally, to their vanished, ceremonial roads.

dune, and canebreak.

and the sudden, wet stitches of a blue hummingbird.

'later, would abandon these sites, and adopt —like their archaic predecessors— an itinerant existence.'

with each death, would burn their hovels; move on.

ghost beads, ghost dances.

Kin Ya'a.

there, where the moon floated, diurnal.

later, towards Gallup, saw, in the flowing chrome, your own features as if pleat and expand.

. . . hair, forehead, teeth. . . .

(like some small collection of ephemeral keepsakes).

each instant, each object, catching, now, in an uninterrupted sequence of displaced frames.

you, who'd match image with image.

who'd bring the disparate twins —the nomadic— to meet, coincide, superimpose.

—the *you,* at last, within the 'you,' inserted—

(that bundle of wild, unkempt rays).

what, scattered, dissipated, held you, now, in a kind of vacuous echo, in the ring of a negative radiance.

(while sleeping in the contours of its scuttled volumes).

further south: mesquite, saguaro.

the minute, electrically-charged signatures of the smallest clouds.

only real, seemingly, what you hadn't yet foreseen.

(the idea, at least, that the word, eventually, might possibly prefigure).

green slag, and the slow lightning, over.

as the desert breaks now into flat, residential sections.

and the traffic gathers —funnels, five lanes— through the unwavering rear-view.

'tokens,' 'keepsakes.'

or a memory run far enough forward that you might, almost fortuitously, encounter some minor, still-emergent feature.

(some vestige, projected).

—a sonorous imprint, resilient enough to hold: withhold you—

for the poem you'd compiled and now nearly completed was still to be written.

still articulated: the length of these relapsing itineraries.

(a syntax equal to all that unhappening).

were so many knuckles, now, studding the black, scalloped steering wheel.

"(some vestige, projected . . .)"

as the tires hiss —slick— down the damp causeways.

rainy city; shiny palms.

V

Of the Four-Winged Cherubim as Signature

FERRARA UNLEAVENED

in memory of my parents

'iodio 131'

1

. . . would wedge this
beneath lids: leave
          messages.   past the last
white orchards, the
winds un-

scaffold.   won't
carry our faces, now, like

some
cherished imprint.   'flourish'
and 'wilt' on a
single

semantic branch.   our
manna's, at
last,

begun falling.   hollow
steps, chisel
dark.   wrap your-

self in
the running gauze of this gutted
script.

2

over and
over, but unto

what?   no image obdurate, brittle
enough to dispel this
dis-
persion.   *sull'Emilia* falls,
keeps

falling, soft onto
wheat, over the
turreted

white
irises and damp,
unplumbed gardens, no
end, no

end to
for-
getting.   sprinkles as it falls. . . .

3

washed,
kept

washing.   that the hair
stream, and the limbs, through the
strung

gutterals.   that
uttered, might
emerge.

~

Ferrara os-
cura. high, over its
vaulted, oven-
dark
doorways, wobbled gold. blossomed, in

a bowl
of

cupped oils. no
end, no
light light, measureless enough, but
that our dead
might re-

member. remember
us. might eye
the

needle to
these dim fires. sip,
from our sonorous jars, our verb
tipped, in-

audible.

~

remember, re-
member us, that the
heart
both crouch and hover, en-

velop these
shadows in a
foam
of sewn bells.

LINEAGE

for my Children

so many voices, there,
vie for the
   voice, crowd sound with the white
pressure of
their

silences.   sea, and the tall
rooms, just

over.   they're
filling, again, with
mirrors, armchairs, my own, as
if

driven, enumerations.   the
'moon' there's the
length

of a
line; the 'vase, with
   its ragged, red dahlias,'
                                        another.

~

trace.   trace
   forwards.   for only

there, eventually, might issue, might
emerge, not as

entities, but as the
   breath's
very imprint, inflection, as
the

still-
moving rumors of the otherwise
ob-

literated.

            ivory, off-white, nacre: I
read them, in
negative.   move,
at their restless extremity, forwards.

~

press, they
press me to say: say 'latch,' 'shutter,'
   the 'jade

ladders' the
angled slats make, once

fastened
against the sea.   ask
that their silences, finally, be
stilled, muted, the sustained bar of the
un-

expiated,
edged.

~

term,
terminalis.   this
  side of

speech, the awnings stiffen; the
charged
barges, running
before the open breakwaters, set
sail.   are

signs, emblems.   are what
there is
as

offering, barter, as the
small, uttered tokens of some momentary
placation.

~

stray
figures.   figments
  of smoke (their muslins,
their
bleached linens wreathed, turbaned in
smoke . . .), we

survive,
survive them, but
scarcely; haul sound, the

tiny
shreds of its
sustenance, forwards.   as if
language
were merely language's edge, its slight,
still-

to-be-
acquitted segment.

move, they're

moving, now,
through knuckles, wrists —the

itinerant
sisters, sporadic

brides. move, they're
moving me to say, say 'jonquil,' 'urchin,'
'kelp.' to feed them
on
the 'small

saline
scraps of the water's reflections. . . .'
figures
from the far

side (even their bracelets, loose
hoops of
smoke), the

oscillum
quavers. the air's
curtain

runs taut. tell them, tell them that the
wind's glowing. that the
prawns, this
summer, abound. that now, towards
dusk, the
pines
are billowing from under. tell them we'd

forgot, that we'd
remembered.   that the

breath, our
breath's vessel, hadn't
rusted.   that, one

by one, the scattered lights of the
low,

offshore islands, the
estuary's, turn
on.

SEVEN ENTRIES FOR A FLORA ON SPEECH

for Paul

the shoots go blond, before
burgeoning. already —it's pre-spring— the
darks shimmer. a phrase, as it emanates,
is sending its tendrils, blind,
through an undergrowth of red mirrors.

---

because, once written, could
continue: trace —past ourselves— the very
first outlines, provisions, for our earliest
rehearsals. nothing, not even the fan of

your fingers, that's not angle, casting, instance. . . .

. . . moved
through my own descriptives. mornings past, in
the opalescence of the still- undeveloped,
drew at
the pleated image. (is the full length that's

meant: its deep flourish and loose,
flagellant releases).

(nereid, or the phrase)

who, by riding back-
wards, blond-eyed and water-
slick, lifts the waves' lids (blown

muscle the least phoneme —riotous— writes against).

---

caught, each time, on the labyrinth
of my own idiom. followed, mistook, re-
traced that thin, ephemeral quiver. there, at
least, was density, resistance. was what the
lightning left, unciphered, through the charred heart
of the laurel.

---

clearer, through my own
waste, followed the low,
scuttled hulls of the nimbus. is
something less, lighter than ourselves that
determines. pulls image —the artifice— free
of its dissolvent mass.

(of the redemptive: a stray vision)

someday, light
as if flooding their very fibers, these tables,
chairs shall fill; the bottles —in
their own, glowing sockets— stand. your voice, its

blown sleeves, no
longer need these 'lyric remissions.'

A FABLE FOR LIGHEA

. . . flew
through sound's dark, dispatched half: the
travelling craters of
its

struck,
still-reverberant surfaces.   lapped
shadows, and the
            low, breath-papered rooms, as they
fade, now,
successive.   (*whose*
muscles, once; whose
lids

held me in the
rolled
folds of image: its in-gathered
                                expanses).

                                no alphabet dense,

com-
pressed enough, now, to
with-
hold us.   would number waves, pebbles.   edge
edges.   draw,
from that

dark
napkin, your
crushed relic, its imprint, a cold,

rose-
coral red.

PORTRAITURE

(Outlines from a Vanishing Baroque)

. . . .
. . . encircled one an-
other with
wet
images.   stuck 'wind' in, and 'hearts.'
stuck 'various
small

ornaments.'   billow, and
wrap; the bundles,
gradually,

get knotted.   our
second lives, in those second worlds (
depth, and
preponderance), dis-
solve.   lighter, now,

drew at the
taut,
ob-

durate drops.   blew, over
your breasts, the very outlines which,
later, they'd
rise in; ripple

to.   were thriving
in the running
folds

of that teased
scenery.   were laying, under
one an-
other's lids, 'light' and 'shadow,' 'the
pale
jade clusters that hang

from the still
flaking *af-*
freschi.'   were, and
weren't.   bunched, weightless, in those
late

perspectives, breathed 'eyes,'
'ankles,' 'your
hair's

smooth
metallic spill. . . .'   beat, to a
bright tissue, these
portraits in which —rhythmic— we'd rise,
shimmering, and
recur.

OF OUR FLORAL SIGN AND ASCENDENT

(Villa di Livia)

. . . rose out of the
thick milk of
those
ruins. hard
buds, and the stiff, wind-

twisted
trumpets of your
scarf. trellis, and

pitch: the
steam
shoots —nacre— through our
drafted

reflections. even our
heart
rises, quilled, into so
many sudden, red
tendrils.

~

Villa
di Livia, and that
garden-
aqueous: pear, laurel,
finch. pierce,
and

sunder. in the
un-

loosened light (your hair, now,
even lighter) your bunched
bracelets
beat.   our mouths
move

under.   *these*
are our
flowers, our high notes, flor-
escent.   this, our
sign, and

ascendent.   on
these, our
fixed

pigments, our
breath
catches, as the
petals stretch —fibrous— and
flare.

VOYAGING SEGMENTS: A FRIEZE

bodies are for flying
to, beating
in (so much space, brought
under, pressed to
the very hollow of its paired releases).

---

way the spray sheathes its own statuary in a flowing gauze of wind-meshed facets.

where, "eating of the same shadows," we'd first appeared.

had swollen into focus.

(our gazes as if catching on the flecked metal of image).

there, where even the darts, running —brushed— through silk, became emblems, blown tokens, to this sequence that, so imperceptibly, had overtaken, and now included us.

drawn us into the narrow, sporadic draft of its octaves.

. . . ovolo, palm-leaf, laurel . . .

light itself, through that ribboned, rococo decor, as if channeled.

---

that, by saying,
ex-
tends, protracts in flat,
conjugated segments the very areas it

evokes.   rolls
number; edges, with its own

fires, the
still-
unconstellated dark.

(a thread as if sipped, consumed by its very needle).

memory, wrapt in muscle, and driven, wedged, into those dense, impacted moments, those rooms that —on entering— dissolve.

(arms pinned, and the hair as if ploughed, either side).

—moved in, through, against one another—

exchanged weights.

for whom the clouds, now, in those high, cavernous pilings, had no consistency other than that which the organs —in their lapping— fashioned, teased forth, conferred.

so many whispers, now, as if honed to a single ray.

(breath folded; knees locked).

a vector, blown 'transitive,' but out of what?   in whose name?   weight-
less, across so much disassembled space. . . .

(the condemned sets of the causal).

carrying within, like a long-tailed coda, the broken data of its own origins.

---

wherein, once, out of
light (in its
ligaments, muscled) the very
first syllables —increments— were ex-
tracted.   were
    pulled, like so

many still-quivering shadows.   a-
    cross the earliest linens, drawn
                                        taut.

---

a grammar of sorts, wrested from the word, and stamped, sequential, into
the thus engendered expanses. . . .

(those very currents —a deep cobalt— we'd sometimes slept in).

what, later, we'd see rising warped into volutes, into those slow, dolorous
attempts —the baroque's— to close rupture, and be wrapt in the coils of
a fresh figuration.

—some yet-unsuspected music of inclusions—

(of everything earth —its fixed stars, unharnessed— had had to relinquish).

as if so much movement, fugacity, might have caught in the complexities of ornament. might have scrolled through the churned creams of its rich, overlapping stuccos.

(turgid lilies, scalloped hearts).

S. Ivo alla Sapienza

where, aside from the echoing, re-entrant bays —their facets, faced inwards— rose, volatilized.

(. . . aside from the paired angels, their hips dimpled in shadow).

driven, already —irrepressibly— past. doomed to the very motion of its own displacements: the polymorph of its phrase.

a syntax, based upon its own dissolutions.

what only the dyads —the drift-rhymes— occasionally, withstood.

(as two orchards, sometimes, paired syncretic).

was what the bodies —in their tall, voyaging portraits—turned towards; closed on.

—the flames wrinkling in that brief sequence of creases—

(just there, then, as the eyes flew backwards).

arms, and the astonishing lightness of a world momentarily delivered, disclosed. ours, among the many, in the froth of its running, effervescent particles.

there as it eddied, like shadow, in the gold corollas of a single, as if scuttled earring.

a wind, too, and along the cracked pediments, a way of leaning, rising, entering so entirely into the instant that the instant as if gathered us into its chords, scales, extended *glissandi*.

a grammar of circumstance turning, as it went, into one of conduit, passage. of the abolished ideation, its luminous, on-going sections.

(what glide, suspended, as if journeying towards the composition of some second, some ultimate sequence).

just then, as the sun, over the ocher suburbs, flattened; set, persimmon.

'hold,' said the hand. and the heart, from the very heart of its decorous metaphor, responded.

irreproachable myth of 'the perfectly mingled . . .'

phrase that floats, as if ghosted. that reaches us, bearing the illegible imprint of those arched, as if lacquered figures, their chins lifted, hair as if shivering to the raised, inexorable movement.

of the now anonymous and entirely engulfed: the slip of living vestige.

that barge we move by.

where, each night, the twin pillows, in lozenge, lay propped, staged for those deep, soundless encounters.

—becoming, as we were, figurants to our own unravelling—

ours, each other's, for as long as our flared, oscillating mirrors lusted after us.

(as, over an armchair, a blouse, poured limply).

—fitted whispers—

there, where only the bodies, seemingly, might still muscle, prod, fashion a shape, a viable form for our passage through.

we, who'd scarcely, yet, appeared.

held, held one another, now, against the bleached, unfeatured expanses of our own dispersion . . .

as if drafted into that late vocable; drawn under.

as a fountain, below, showered its pale, slate-blue figures in its piled, overhanging plumage.

a nymph —slick— against its indolent splatter.

nothing, not even the least, wind-beaded drop, in that piped effusion, that wasn't, as it arced, as if ligated.

Breaths' Burials

for Eliot Weinberger

I

On the Fragility of Idols

AS IF WRITTEN IN A BOOK OF GLASS

for Sarah & Charlie

. . . as if written
in a
book of glass, read

of so
many sunken
numbers, eyes

fluttering like
fish at
the

base of
the
world.   there, what-

ever issued, only
re-
entered, in-

extricable as
wind, but
viscous,

ballasted, the
heart as
if walking on its

head.   was there a
way, asked
the word of the

word?   memory
flooded, and lust
too

sudden, counted corals,
rep-
licated beads, while the

breath, hesitant,
hung be-
tween syllables.

ODE ON THE ELABORATION OF INTERVAL

. . . the same wave
that
fed, once, on its own
   unraveling, all mica now, and
schist.   ground heart, the

dark organs
of

image.   had gradually
emerged, come
crawling
   from under, gathering   —in my
crossed arms—   my very
own

shoulders.   planks and
clapboard, our
quick

identifications, each thing
so
indissociably it-
self, self-
imbued.

~

even air, the air e-
bullient, the
ac-

cessibility, now, of
all matter, those
massive
ap-

propriations.   (worked only
for the
disparate, that part —the dark slip
  of muscle, the fanned shadow
of lashes— which had
no
equivalence.   which held, held
us, just

out of
reach).

~

was, it
  would seem, like a running curtain,
nearly a
world.   (there were, we knew, no

others).

~

out, onto the
windy stage of
  our landscapes, would wheel clouds,
trundle

en-
tire cartloads of
replica.   gods, too, in *trompe l'œil,* the
whole
spectacle of the

pre-
empted.   nothing's
too far, it
would seem, if —in flaking— it

re-
flect.   if, spoken,
re-

sound.

~

whereby 'would,'
'might,' the lost
panoply
of the conditional.   yes, that even
  here, within the
lens

of my own
breath, 'you' —of
all
words, the very
first— might, at last, issue.   be
blown

over the
bright pages.   brought
to that luster, those shadows, these
rocks that glisten
in the very
lee
of their own saying.   to where, that
is, sub-

stance it-
self

might substantiate.

~

(no, it's
not me, now,
who's being illusive, but the overwhelming
im-
mediacy of each
vacated instant.   the surfeit

of so
much
scuttled letter).

~

be sign and
its ef-
fluence, the draft of your
scarf, as —al-

ready— it
enters interval.   there, just
   over the
ocean's
grey echo, gather buttercup
and rue, bindweed and gentian.   give to
each —each instance— its

own
measure.   for breath

against breath, it's
through the words we'd
accede: phrase
you
initiate, and I —in diastole— pursue.

FOURTEEN IRISES FOR J.L.

there, blossoming once again, like blown
goblets, the irises in their annual
ovulations. yes, emptiness, at
last, enveloped, inscribed. is there anything, indeed, but
emptiness? but emptiness, at last, en-
veloped? inscribed?

. . . one color
follows upon another like
polyphonic voices: last week, violet, and
this, a rubbed mahogany, freckled rose, recalling
worlds —voices— you've never known.

. . . like so
many stubby paintbrushes, they
burst —turbaned— into splashed
panels, running murals (a breath as
if perishing in the
very exercise of its scales).

---

no, it's not the irises that
return, each spring, but
ourselves. ourselves —cyclical— who've entered the
sign, and stoop, now, before
them: tenuous altars to our own
tenuous passage.

---

all irises, finally,
kaleido-
scopic; with each
in-
finitesimal turn, a
fresh

conceit. god-
blossom, lightning-

root, verb on which,
germinal, the
air it-

self's as if
ir-
idized.

---

like those glazed, in-
voluted tissues on their tall, un-
wavering stems, we, too, as if
perch, alighting —as we have— amongst phonemes,
polyphones: what tell us, each
instant, to our fingertips.

---

came late. even later, now, *la*
langue d'oc having all
but vanished, remained the irises, the troubadours'
lightning roses, blue
as thunder in the dark thunder's
dissoulucioun.

---

where dew slips,
icy
pearl, from its

petal, the
tall stalk

scarce-
ly trembles. . . .

---

irises, really, are nothing more
than the frozen frames of an otherwise
invisible drift, our relentless
elision past.   what they —heraldic,
voluptuous— would arrest.

---

how each of these blossoms —these
volutes— lapping ogival, in-
scribe a void.   oh ours, that hollow, that
heart, that inherent omission: doom blooming
from the rhizomes up.

---

drafted, the petals get blown, now,
across paper.   their deep
scrolls, rolled tabernacles, little more
than scribbled deposits.   chimeric hoards.

(*gothic*)

death, and these,
our ever
more
ephemeral re-

sponses, their
fluttering
chalices (faience
the

skull dreamt. . .).

. . . way that the irises drift, now, be-
neath yours.   current in which —wind-
barges— they'd enter, perhaps, your
very dreams.   there, before dissolving (so much
grammatical particle) might billow.   writhe vibrant.

---

a white chair, its legs caught
in tall stalks
of white iris, was what, finally,
remained.   monologue in which, abandoned
to those immensities, each
of us murmur.

PSALMODIC

knelt there, in that
knuckle of
rock.   nothing's
less than the word, brittle
as

crumbs, not
even the wind, what's
rising —gentian— just now,
be-

fore you.

TRANSPARENT ITINERARIES: 1991

were no origins (so we were told), only ends.

nowhere, really, to reach except those occasional places in which, sometimes, we'd orchestrate those ends. set their emptiness —in measured bars, volutes, ellipses— to sound.

those hill villages, for instance, each autumn, weeks after they'd been abandoned.

still, after so much depredation, an ocherous rose.

language, making metaphor as it does out of a fundamentally metaphoric existence, has —at least— the power of its double negations.

'you,' it would seem, more *place,* at first, than *person.* (there, for example, where the shadows —in foaming— as if seethed).

existing, as we did, in so much myriad reflection.

—flamboyant shell—

---

nearer, certainly, you would have
vanished; further, we'd
                    never have known
that —for hours at a time— we'd
                                        had the same name.

---

otherwise, endless as the air itself.   as wind, the consistency of soot.

only the glint, you said, wasn't incidental.   only the glint, occasionally, glowed (or seemed to).

'seemed to,' I repeat, observing —thus— that spent usage.

—you, who'd always been just an instant earlier—

---

within your gaze, would
    turn; in your long fingers,

root.

---

composed, as we are, of creases.   of creases and appendages.   or so, at least, we'd assumed.

oh, how many hallucinated cells within a single, predetermined body.

. . . the mirage of how many rocks . . .

where a distance —once— preserved us.

kept us primed —as if essential— within its invisible quiver.

(what, awakened, the organs first rose toward).

its icons invested with breath: *our breath.* what held us —for so long— out of reach of our own dismantling.

flexed interval.

what, with each new appropriation, had only receded. had nearly vanished, now, into an 'already-after'.

worn tokens; gutted sums.

'seeking to conquer a larger liberty, man,' according to Melville, had but extended 'the empire of necessity.'

. . . in which, not even gagged, a gratuity of sounds . . .

---

would wrestle in
   these shadows for that
light, that
luster, for those
blown drops driven —incandescent— past so
much extinguished
mirror.

---

as if cupped, irrecuperable.

an alcove in air!

where, otherwise, had gone on vanishing in the very midst of so much acquisition: at the very heart of its heavily compressed metals.

mother of no one, as
woman you
enter, occupy nothing, but stand, water-
slick in the midst of these pitted
whispers, no one's, once
again.

ANGUISH & METAPHOR

only in air
  do the knots dissolve, only
without, with-
in, in the echoing

organs, dis-
perse. earth in-

verted, a life as if passed
a-
mongst its
attributes, you'd rise,
rise as

I'd plummet, your hair —in-
voluted— harden, just
there, where

I'd
vanish.

TRACING A THIRST

for E.F.

called it: tracing a
thirst, the poem
as it

sluices a
passage; with each,
dry

utterance, edges
towards its
own

ob-
fuscated source.   no,
not the

world, the
world's, but,
per-

haps, its
very
postulate.   what the

winds
would lap, and the
tongue,

ultimately,
muscle: breath, like
so

many
empty bubbles, brought
to

that pleated lip.

THE VILLAS OF ANDREA PALLADIO

there, once again, at the
  world's
very edge, you're
pointing out palaces, aren't
you?   tapping

at that viscous
glass, holding them, the
im-

memorabile, at the
tip

of your lacquered
nail.   there, just there, where the
barge pivots, seems to
station in the
midst

of its own vapors.   'see
it?' you

ask.   I see
your lacquered nail, its
wavering
reflection, follow it

across
those stalled waters.   *pier, pilaster,*
fronton, the pure scale

of so much
hal-

lucinatory mass.   (not even a
hedgerow to break
the

effect, not even
a stray dog, the ragged line of
its
leash).

~

null, in so
many
numbers, isn't this
   what you mean?   this, that's
meant?   blown
mirrors, the void in

which, turgid, our
viscera

would glow?   among the
room,
rooms, the
words empty —spacious— enough to

withhold us?   isn't
this, that's
nothing, what the
   cells —wedging— would jam?

~

billows about you, a
scarf of
clouds, pigeons.   yes, a sudden
air
of apparent be-

wilderment.   tell, tell
me to my-

self, before even
you
get swept
into that wash of sounds, the lagoon,
al-

ready, in a
sputter
of tugs, marked by so

many rigorously
a-
ligned pilings.   yes, before
our own breath hardens
a-

bout its very
words, and our bodies, once again,
beat

against the
muslin of their veiled reflections.

ON THE NATURE OF THE ICONIC

what bursts in the very moment of bursting is image.

its bunched chimera.

even though, immediately after, she'd as if begun gathering together her every gesture; as if collecting —once again— the scattered, grey blades of her gaze.

accumulating —as you'd put it— diaphanous.

just there, where the curtains ripple, each time, through the draft of their own deafness.

neither this side, nor that.

(of what, indeed, knew no end, no depth, no dimensions whatsoever, but —being verbless— existed in an underworld entirely its own).

a well of shadows —you might have written— surrounded by a garland of splashing leaves.

by the gloss of so much apparent matter.

while she —steadily— as if thinned into focus.

(fixed rays of her earrings; what she'd just fastened, sapphire).

muscled, luminous.

as if such signs (in an uninterrupted emission of signs) might only have erupted out of the disarticulated. its depths.

cast in so much counterpart.

she, as if reconstituting that white memory to which you'd otherwise have had no access.

miming its exact outlines, its deepest cleavages.

toying, thus, with those immemorial losses, thoroughly unaware, in so doing, of the magnitude of such provocation.

the tips of her fingers, that very instant, running nimble over her glowing cheeks; adjusting here, there, the slightest wires of that all-too-perfect dissemblance.

like notes, struck vibrant, off some dismantled instrument.

yes, just then, as her each feature converged. grew limpid.

the circumstantial, absolute.

oh, all the meanings, values, irrefutable definitions we'd given ourselves.

the alphabets. the blown letters of how many driven alphabets.

(within which, notwithstanding, had adored).

as she stood there, now, her name changing with the light, the shadows, the
time of day: pure replica of the otherwise obliterated.

as if the door alone might be altar.   our very last.

and the moment itself, sacrificial.

IDIOM

no work, now,
   for the living, had risen on so
many scuttled
images.   euphoria, a
form

of despair, spoke
only

to the mouth, shoving
'clouds'
between its teeth, slipping 'mineral.'
"still there?"
would

ask, as if the lips, alone,
might sprout, break florescent
into their
own

abolished
idiom.

NACRE

dawn, and the ground as
  if slipping
from under-
neath the brittle sheath of its stars:
all those
in-

nate in-
stabilities. what the 'given,' each

time, took. told us (just as you'd
tell your-
self) that the body's
bundled, the nerves knotted
about something far too slight, e-
vanescent, to

utter. lay it, then, in the
interstice: *between* the
be-

tween. oh all
that e-

laborate scroll, the white
letter of
protracted allusion: the
name alone of the figure you'd glow in,
nacreous, now, in the

flagellated rays of
its nimbus.

THE DEATH OF FLASH-BACK

no, not even those
  wind-
pitted belfries, their quarried rectangles scooped
into so
many minuscule
alveoli, no, not even they, now,
would receive
notice.   faster, the

instant as
if ob-

literates its own
passage, feeds
us

on its fresh
vacuities.   arms, shoulders, teeth: *these,* after
all, were our
last

possessions.   were what
we'd

wager
against that
very sleekness.   for enveloped, the
breath, occasionally, still went under.   took us

into the
heavy folds of
its mirrors: there, where
  beds, carpets, armchairs stood, like

salvage itself,
within its rippling pleats.   wedged, would

lie there, our gazes
blown, while our lives, as
if

voided, flew
over.

II

Lines from Pietro Longhi

". . . and the floor by the girl, rendered darker."
P.L., 13 May 1749

for Beatrice & Beatrice

. . . here, sheets
of music
have as if
  fluttered onto the
vermillion
table, where the
three
musicians, squinting,
inter-
pret whatever bars
that they
can.

. . . in the midst
of so much black
crinoline, she's
curtsying
be-
fore the
beige lady, the
tip
of whose fan
poses circumspect
a-
gainst an
intransigent chin.

. . . here, only
empty
gesture, infatuated
deed.   with the
brief
sweep of
a hand, he's
showing her
towards the tall,
chocolate-
brown volumes, his
eyes, all the
while, fixed
upon the
deep
heave of her bosom.

. . . with fans
like black
scallops
half-
covering their
face, they
traffic in
whispers (the
thin
lascivious hiss
of so
much strict
con-
fidenze).

. . . appears twice in
the same
painting (she, even
creamier in the
oval
portrait that
Longhi, just to the
left, executes,
his
brush, that
very
instant, lingering
a-
gainst the gold fold
of her
lid).

---

staring into a
future that they'd
never see, these
svelte
extortionists, masked
as-
trologi.

---

she's reading her
own
wretched fortune
into the
palm
of the plump
bellezza, who's
gazing —for
her
part— into the
deep
reaches of some
pale
arborescent decor.

. . . the tiny dogs
in the paintings of
Pietro
Longhi are
no less ornamental
than his
sitters.   most
wear
ribbons, usually
cerulean, sometimes
cold
rose.

. . . against a
floor, lacquered
black, the
scattered
flotilla of their
narrow,
ivory-
white slippers,
each set, it would
seem, at
some critical, pre-
determined
angle.

---

behind the
black moon of her
  mask, she
no longer
needs
her mirror, only
the gaze of
her
appraiser: what
looms, just
now, massive,
be-
tween the pinched
line of her
lids.

. . . leads her,
her
voluminous
skirts, over a
floor scattered
with
playing
cards, whispering
endearments,
urging,
ca-
joling her as they
go.

. . . up, and some-
what to
the left, a puppet's
seen ap-
plauding those
poised
figures, their
fans laid
flat
a-
gainst a
billowing froth of
oyster-
white ruffle.

. . . in the *ritratto*
di famiglia, the
utter
isolation of
each
member, rigid
as
enamel
chessmen, a draft
as if
wrapping each in
the aura
of some self-
infatuation.

. . . a whole,
closed
universe, in which
   no one
acknowledges
an-
other, where even
their
glances —sparse,
furtive, a-
skew— appear
as
if gloved.

. . . with faces, like
porcelain
ovals, they
stare —from their
dark
parlors— into the
only
light, now,
that's left: ours
with our
passing
off-
handed appraisals. . . .

III

The Densities of Naught

". . . there is no numberless number in the malady of time."

". . . became pregnant with Nothing."

Meister Eckhart

PREFACE

might have ended here, at the
  very outset, fruit
bobbing white
be-

fore your very
eyes, the clouds, the
fat
skeins of the prophetic, yet

un-
scrolled.

A PORTRAIT WITHOUT FEATURES

. . . no, not from what you'd
said, but
murmured, had
grown.   grown beautiful, abundant, now,
be-

fore your own
dis-

solutions, bringing your
body, at last, to the
sheer

weightlessness
of
each breath.   isn't this what's
meant?   this

transliteration
of every part?   the lymph-at-
last-in-
ef-

florescence?

hunch, now, a-
gainst nothing.   roll your shoulders
   over the vaporous bulk
of so much
pillow, letting your
teeth

feed deep
up-
on their very lips.   if the windows, this
instant, blew open, they'd

never
close.

ENTRY

every entry, you
   write, is invisible.   write, then,
about rocks, the bright
syllables that
stud them.   'away,' in fact, is always

nearer, and
nearer yet, that

wild swarming, those gold cells, the
deposits your
breath would make
   over the clamped lids of the naught. . . .

LAMP

nights, would
   channel loss, feed
upon its
taut corollas, burgeoning, as we
did, about the

nihil, the
nullitas-
e-

bullient.   called it 'ex-
emption,' the
end

of metaphor, its
dark oils
fueling
no one's light along light's

very
edge.

TRANSCRIPT

carried it, like
   some vestigial gland, those sound-
less particles.   puffs
of

dust, what the
fingers
would cup, that dark, e-

jaculated light.   'world,' you'd called
it, what lay, just
be-

yond.   there, your eyes as
   if rising out
of
their own
buried negative, would meet, in the very

same
instant, their speckled
mirrors.

TEATRO

sped, each time, into
   emptiness, gathering as we did —re-
flexive— against the
on-

coming naught.   taut, the
tendons, the

raw curtains drawn
onto our own
re-

leases.   what if room, the
scuttled bracelets and strewn shoes
were
nothing more

than so much
decor?   and ourselves, massed in
motion, but the
figurants

of some abstract
en-
actment?

                              no, not nothing, had written,
but *nothing*, and our limbs,
nimble, swimming
towards.

TRANSPARENT ITINERARIES: 1992

air, air-
  infinite, your
very
last obstacle, into
which, wreathed in grain, steadily
                                        as if receded. . . .

---

you, who'd poured shadow over the white pages; who'd renounced, now, all claim to literality.

where, through the knuckles of the dead anemones, a mute idiom as if drifted . . .

wanting only what you'd never, entirely, articulated.

what, uttered, you might —finally— address.

---

just there, where, hallucinatory, the
light
slipped liquid . . .

---

having wandered —as you had— through your own rumors like some life-sized rendering set in the midst of so much alien decor.

the quinces, you wrote, had gone golden. dimpled like a cherub's buttocks, they reminded you, didn't they, that 'there' was still 'there.'

quintessential, that *one remove.* what more, in fact, had you ever asked for?

where, like a beryl, would lie —deeply inserted— at the very heart of your own projections.

that apophatic night.

immensely empty, immensely moving.

(waiting for that moment in which, indeed, all memory would end).

. . . otherwise, had traveled that far
only to
film mineral, the
eye, an alveolus of wind, shadow, of so much
skittering

  guesswork. thinned as you
went, your mouth as

if gagging on its
own
echoes.

---

oh the sheer inertia of so much mirror!

sought verticals —updrafts— amongst the ever more impacted masses.

would, with so many white, scorching pellets, rid yourself of your own fatality, if you could, within the viscera of some elected 'other.'

---

whose scarf,
scarlet, would be
   light enough, seemingly, to
in-
hale.

---

the divine, you knew, was never more than the nominal substitute for those wordless expanses.

the dark daisy-chains of the *nicht.*

would go on surviving yourself, wouldn't you, in those bright interstices: under their slapping, wind-struck lattices.

---

on the
'no' of
that mumble, its thin
meats, gnaw.

---

where, otherwise, through so much sonorous waste, the stars —elephantine— only went on growing.

DOMINO

no, not for the
   words, but for that ephemeral
nudge-
syllable, the
nihil as if glittering

just be-
yond.

ABSOLUTION

whereby, charged
   with emptiness, would pour
the sounds back, find
for

each herb, its
voided
counterpart.   a language-with-
out, that the breath, at
last, might absolve

its least
syllable; the twisted conch, the
vault

of its muffled
fountain.

ARTICLE OF FAITH

through its drafts —conduits— the
   poem unnames you as it goes.   isn't that
what you'd
sought: so many facets, laid —at
last— into that damp,
redundant
tomb.

POĒSIS: A CONCEIT

only there, through the
  lyric-
eviscerals, would you enter: your
each feature, in its
empty

mirrors, at
last, reflect.   a

life-without, you'd
called it: the
seething granary of the heart, in
so

many meted sections, sieved, dis-
patched.

                    the null: the null, at
last, ebullient.   and
you, little

more than this body you'd
tease —mass,
cajole— through the narrow stalk of
so

much
muttered syllable.

A PORTRAIT OF SORTS IN MID-MARCH

high over the charred bars of the
   vineyards, a
moon sips
at its own lozenge.   you, too, as
if

thin, self-
dissolve, leaving little more, now,
than that mask you'd
made, its

breathing sheaths: what you'd tapped,
fashioned, perforated into
some-

thing so utterly transparent that
not even you, now,
needed to

ad-
mit to yourself.   bulk without
body, moving over the
burnt

thistles, had you reached, at long
last, the

perfect consistency?   the same weight
as the weeds?   as the
onion stalks you'd
offer —that

very instant— to the abolished face
of the
in-
visible?

BREATHS' BURIALS

. . . wasn't burial
what you'd meant, the breaths'
   re-
current tombs?   jars, those cherished
vessels, what first

had brought you, still
stammering, into
that late

hiatus.   rings, circles, the
pathetic attempt at
some
illusory circum-

scription.   what rushes, rushes wordless, now,
towards its very
heart.   there,
as the

string snaps, the opals, in the same
instant, would
spill.

ECKHART

. . . sacred, once, where
we'd vanished, reappearing, as
we would, no-
where.   no-

where, now, vanished no-
where (the
door

within the
cloud, we'd

learnt, had dissolved semantic).
beat dust, shook
wind.   down

through the
fresh
definitions, as if funneled.   *here,*
we're told, *every-*
thing's, at

last, here.   we, who'd
sipped
fire, fed
on interval, rummaged, now, a-
mongst our own

dull
vestige.

VENDANGE

. . . with autumn, the
vineyards lay
like rolled, baroque jewelry.   was earth, but
only

in interstice, in its
narrowest passages.   weren't the
eyes, those
cherished relics, looking for their own, lost

portrait?   molding the air
to that abolished
anatomy?

enter, but
where?   feed, but on what?   teased to a squint,
heard the breath press
on those swollen
gold
clusters.

·

SAINT VÉRAN

towards the very end, remained
miracles, didn't
there?   those

reliquiae in which, webbed, ir-
idescent, dragons
still

slept.   oh, would blow
over
every knuckle, over each

heated
pebble.   for world's, first, what
isn't.   that, swollen

within our own shadows, we
release —this
time— those

laminated scales, our
syntax, hal-
lucinatory.

TRANSPARENT ITINERARIES: 1993

we pretend to be here, don't we? and sometimes, perhaps, we really are. but only drawn, drafted: in the very instant of our own extrications.

ocher splattered across the facing parapets . . .

or, occasionally, in the pollenization of certain syllables.

within, that is, the *without.*

the sheer physicality of being alive, but only then: in those buoyant, wind-driven intervals.

the breath —that very instant— giving birth to the lips.

(*verb*)

what had taken forever, it
seemed, to
reach you, carried you, now, in the
throe
of your own utterance past.

---

bodies without flesh, flesh without bodies: yes, but there, in the blue cradle of those hollow relocations: the passage.

as the phrase itself as if narrowed to a fresh omission.

coned, elusive.

while each feature in the portrait vanished —seemingly— within the blind perspective of so much damp, overlapping foliage.

organized as we are about a certain naught.

—an empty ore—

ended, kept ending, wouldn't stop —you wrote— the imminence of our endings.

(*either*)

mirror pressed to its
   last
unctuous drop, you turn, turn
back, keep wondering
which of
us
will be aureoled, finally, in the other's ash.

---

sealed yourself in with signs: with 'lips,' 'forehead,' 'throat;' in a quarantine of tiny, breath-bitten utterances, subsisted.

for whole months at a time, inhabited a book that would never be written.

—swarming of silence about the charmed annunciates—

so incredibly far to encounter, finally, those sensuous indemnities: what lay, each time, even further.

---

imagined her, her
   entire body as if ventilated by
letter (she who'd
written: "if I await consequence
nothing will

end," ends in passage, your
eyes'
relentless entries).

---

there, in that distant body, your deepest ear.

even now, at the very edge of metaphor, of each earthen composite, were drawn by the *wasn't* into an indissociable *would.*

dust, dust and petal in the elasticity of inference.

—members tensed—

where from the mesh of so much fluffy, evanescent gauze as if sipped.

THE GAZE

fixed, insistent, over so
  much fluttering reflection (water jugs,
flower pots) the gaze e-

licits its
own
response.   field, that field-

reverberant (were there, in-
deed, any others?).   was what, welded in
air, the air's a-
lone, we'd

tug.   tear at.   savage
for the sake of
so
very little.   you move —boy's head— as
if it were me, that

sheath.   and
me, as if your body, but those blown, o-
palescent rivets.   yes, each of us
as
if draining the

other for
what's —after all— neither's.

AN AFTERLIFE

through one another, rushed
  phantasmagoric.   there, where the
hips scissored and the
thick

hair streamed, mimicked, didn't
we, the

gestures of the
living.   too sudden (even for
our-

selves) how the air sipped, lip-
hard, about
our
ankles; worked

at our hands, shoulders; as if in-
haled our each,
echoing

organ.   drawn
across the entire breadth of its
dis-

assembled spaces, had entered the
intervals, what
drifted —dissolute— in
continuous

ex-
pansion.   yes, there, in that
afterlife

of our own making, where the very
letters —the
alphabet itself— as if floated in

broken
constellations, would cling, wouldn't
we, to those scattered
sections. wrap —desolate— a-
bout so much

billowing scaffold:
hold

to whatever volutes still
held, it
would seem, the least promise of some
minor, al-
together fortuitous
re-

location.

DARK DRAFTS: THE PREPOSITIONS TOWARD

never doubted that you were after your own undoing, but only at the hands of those —the adored— who'd already undergone theirs.

whose hearts —like beautiful faces— faced backwards.

bearing as they did, like blank stigmata, the signs of that cryptic omission.

—were like whispers, you say, without words, issuing from a mouth without memory—

void's particulars.

(what the weather, in its coiled chambers, would rush towards).

as if we could only complete ourselves within the deepest recesses of those on the very verge of departure.

indeed, each other's unearthing.

who'd draw us —rhythmic— through their thinning inhalations.

their viscera, alone, as if vectorial.

wind, light, the very shadows of a world that no one, entirely, returned from.

we who'd shed identity like so many armored scales, but only for the sake of that sudden gust: for the dark draft of its fortuitous reflections.

shivering crystals in which —at last— we'd recognize our own anonymity.

their gaze both the icon and candlelight with which it's incrusted.

the grey, you'd discovered, was flecked green. words —observations— such as this took on all the properties, now, of relic.

as had the shadow of the ankles themselves.

as if our very fortunes had been cast, irrevocably, within the narrows of so much seeming ephemera.

words as residue.

the vocable itself nothing more, finally, than the shell of so much vanished delectation.

say that the mirror, in fact, hadn't reflected but absorbed. drawn us —irresistibly— past.

initiates to the air's immeasurable asymmetry.

tracing as we went that vapor —that very darkness— to the extent of our own depletion.

(was nowhere, finally, but *there*).

IV

Odes of Estrangement

FIRST ODE: ALREADY AFTER

for the pages of the
voice
vanish, fast as
they're turned.   liquescent, the

very
same spaces, just
after: their glistening

residue.   what
toads or
the fat calyx of
certain marsh flowers still, some-
times,

exuded.   had
stopped talking, telling one an-

other each
other's name, the
contours, the exact volumes our
sleep
had taken.   asked yourself, occasionally,
'still there?' as your brow

rising through the
bright

oval, came to meet
the black
liner.

~

had let, let
one

another out, hadn't we, and
found the
im-

mensity, beyond, some-
how
smaller.   was wind, though, and the un-
mistakable scent, every-

where, of salt.   of salt-
pervasive, as if
reclaiming the
very
least cavity, indentation, of

memory it-
self.   crowding it,
vacuous.

~

'avocet,' you'd still,
oc-
casionally, as
if interject, pointing out (a relic in
it-

self) that elegant stilt, its
beak, an
up-
turned tendril.

(while the word itself

flew forward, a
pawn
on some illegible board, to enter, al-
ready, the
al-

ready-
after).

SECOND ODE: PASTORALE

written, the
words
become anyone's, no one's.
wouldn't need you,
now, the

flowering
fruit-

trees, what
you'd scribbled, in white
bars, across so

much
mute scoring.   on that

broken
ground, its
raised chords, wouldn't even

need your-
self.

THIRD ODE: SAINT URSULA, VENICE

her dream, frozen in
ocher pigments, had set yours
a-
drift.   so little, now, to

keep you, the
stays, the
moorings fast to their
own
wobbling reflections.   bit by
bit, had

worked free, hadn't
you?   broken 'miracle' into so
many constituent

parts.   weren't
these, indeed, our

last relics, the
petal and
fracture?   the pieces that still, some-
how, with-
stood?

                    swarm, then, to
what?   for the
sections themselves as if long

for deployment.   your
breath, to bud

in the very
midst
of the fresh numbers.   alternately, you
are and
aren't, depending on the sounds

you'd employ.   no matter
how

sham, tenuous, the
kind of paradise —murmured—
you'd pro-
ject.

FOURTH ODE: EURYDICE

through the mirror's
very
heart, had run
shafts, hollowed corridors.   saw you,
raw as

hair, perched
with-

in its
deepest cell.   spoke, because you
couldn't.   rolled you, supple
as
your own
shadows, over the lip of

so
much stasis.   these,
then, were the words, the

offerings
of the
open, the empty, of the thoroughly
ex-
tricated.

~

who, then,
in this vacuous
ballast

would save whom?   through the late
drafts, driven currents, your
ankles
quiver, quick

as fish.   here, where the
mouth draws

on memory alone; where
bulky, pendulous, each organ
weighs
exactly that

of a
breath.

~

but no.   there's
no one, nothing, you
your-

self might have echoed.   but the
light as it shifts
over so much
idle
decor.   you, whose least glance

makes a ladder, a
scale

unto an octave in which, heap
of whispers, the instrument
itself

won't even
be

husked.   nor its
innumerable
parts,
methodically shredded.

FIFTH ODE: POTENTIA

. . . followed yourself
through your own, displaced
worksites (whole
weeks in
the white scaffolds of a single,
   refractory sound).   yours, these

arms, organs
a-

waiting conveyance: the
buoyancy of some
exact
syllabication.   doves, juniper, the
bright

lime quarries, just over.   isn't this
what you'd worked towards?   the
world, the world's, the very
magnitude

you'd thin to? wedge,
trans-

parent?

~

whereby the
dahlias, gargantuan, their red petals
un-

dulant as octopi.   whereby the
air, the

uttered air, what you'd
bring, in
measured increments, through all
that

dep-
redated space.   (*there, in that*
late country, you'd no longer
be
yours.   you, who'd

already have reached, by then, the 'may,' the
'might,' the ever-
narrowing
coils

of some tenuous
'could').

SIXTH ODE: THE GROTTOES

is always towards the furthest, and,
  finally, towards the
lost themselves that the senses transit, slip
furtive. that bunched in
muscle, we'd

lusted, it seems, after so
very

little. channels, conduits, the
  secret history —perhaps— of history it-
self, written
in

dark drafts, elusive
scribbles. as if, inadmissible, mass in its
very
densities, were
riddled. and you, nothing more

than this breath
that edged. tongue that
in-

sinuated.

~

                    oh eyes so pale, you'd
written, they'd
promised grottoes. oh holy, the

grottoes, the hollows, the weird birds of
our own,
dis-

articulated heart.   (what, in
de-

fault, had
been plundered,
re-
lentless).

~

                                        'an earth, but else-
where,' isn't this
what you meant?   what you'd say?   what the
eyes rising —yes, so pale,
   so
impervious— already divulged?   for *here's*
only here in the vocable's
forced

re-
tention.   past, past
ourselves, in our own, sonorous dis-

persions, resonates the
gloriole, the
ring

of things released.   the rocks, just
now, as if a-
float

in the puddle of their own shadows, and the
papery, pink blossoms of the
cistus, rife

with light, with the very
light, it would

seem, of some ultimate
ac-
quittance.

~

massed, now,
a-
long the edges, awaited —you'd written— no,
not the barge, the puffed
barge, but the

particle.   but the
predicate, be-

fitting.

                                        yes, holy the grottoes, the
hollows, those extricated worlds which
lie, luminous with
sound, there —just
there— past the inviolable lines of
our own
fore-

closures.

SEVENTH ODE: THE RELICS

. . . as if chained
to those clouds —what billowed
against the blind walls of your forehead— sought
losses, didn't you?   those elaborate
  excavations in which, unearthing less,
ever lesser, only kept
what you hadn't
found.

relics, what the
breath, once,
had buried.   had enveloped
in so much verbiage, the still-
  drifting digits —nimbi— of the in-
dissociable.   would traffic, wouldn't

you, in
those omissions.   in that much
empty

imprint.   you, living
as you did, towards the very end, at the
earth's

virtual completion, rummaged, didn't
you, a-
mongst those spent
sonorities.   there, just there, within
systems so dense, so perfected (their only attributes,
themselves) picked, didn't

you, at that
syntactic
trash.

~

oh hollow, you
wrote, the heart's a
hollow, a hole in which, a window in

which, a cloud in
which, in

which nothing, really, but, occasionally, some occasional hiatus, really, a 'where' whereby a small smattering of rays, perhaps, might alight, occasionally, like in some kind of pantoscopic vision, might even, through the medium of some artifice, like a kind of spray, say, pelt the heart, putting it to rest, momentarily, with something unlikely as a smile so dolorous, so beatific, you'd swear that what you'd just witnessed was not only real, but real in such a way that nothing, in fact, could ever again presume to such consummate reality, notwithstanding the fact that, occasionally. . . .

and so on, etc.,
etc.   for in the name of
nothing, had

reached
this abundance.   in the name of name, finally,
this nominal
diktat.

~

'scoop,' you'd whisper, and
   feel your lips
curl to the
injunction.   for under, just under, as if
buried in
sacks, soft as
organs (the sacks themselves
jingling dully with their own, un-

recycled waste) would lie the first,
banished strata.
would

lie, that is, that iridescence, the puffed
vapor of some long-
since
discarded compound.   'scoop,' you'd murmur, would
hear your-

self murmur, as time after
time, would plunge

through that
wasted idiom.   would
poke —wouldn't you— through so much scroll, the
un-
rolled print-outs of some post-

historic in-
fallible.   oh less, so much less, even
less than the refuse you'd
worked through, would
lie, at

last, that broken
vo-

cable.   oh worthless as
wind, as light itself, would it slip, ineffable,
from your fingers?   would it?   from the
claw your
fingers formed as
they'd pick, jab, grapple at its
very

edges?   oh blown weather,
dis-

banded heart, whatever utters,
utters nothing, really.   and makes of that
nothing —lyric— its
only
measure.

Towards the Blanched Alphabets

I

Under the Bright Orchards

GENESIS

from the very outset, a
needle, a
no-thread,
run inextricable
through the living mass. flared, then

guttered, that
ore, that either, that *isn't* that

is. wasn't this
what you'd flex to, sink
through: gaze so much lighter than all
the

oleander it ever
lingered
in?

UNDER THE BRIGHT ORCHARDS

for M. W.

. . . ink's for the
phosphorous white eyelets, for sprinkling the
pages with
blown
phonemes. a counterworld, you'd

called it: an erratic calligraphy
of
hatched shadows (*was what*
had brought us, carried us, in dark drafts, a-
cross the
vaporous landscapes of the
rigorously

pre-
scribed). a squiggle, then, for the
first hornet, pale
tracery

for the rush, clustering, of
bud. does it curl, will it catch? wrap us, this
very instant, in the
folds of our

own dictation? here, here's
a
dash, and there, the scooped hull of some sudden
imperative. drags, now,
in deep loops, our

hearts under, holds us in the
spell of
its running numbers. rocks, walls, the laddered
light: what the knuckles,
a-

lone, substantiate. passage, a passage, at
last, through the blanched
im-

measurable. yes, here, in a shiver of
blossoms, gloss of
winds, draws us —in
the
hollow coil of our own dark scribbles— past.

THE EMPTY ALPHABET

for M. O'B.

you inhale them, the
    hills, find yourself uttering in
tense
segments the ledges, the brittle gold
of the oaks. an
earth effusive, but only

in its letters, the
breath's

transparent coinage. you
who'd spend, if you could, even your-
self,
setting hands, heart, hair to those all
but ob-

solescent measures. oh burst
world, blown
whispers, who'd feel,
finally, your whole body harden to
an

orifice of
air.

PREMISES

as if all language were rooted in the silent grammar of an implication.

deriving from, and —inseparably— referring to.

as if, indeed, there were two languages: our own, perfectly audible, articulate, appreciable, and another —uninterruptedly mute— which is never more than the taut, vibratory surface of the implicated.

but the *frappe* of so much white letter.

what our own words aspire, reach towards, as if to imbue themselves with the sonorous luster of their own origins.

. . . in, say, a sheer coincidence of mass . . .

what we can only qualify (bound as we are to analogy, metaphor, conceit) as their confiscated mirror.

as an etymology of sorts abolished in the exact same instant as its formulation.

for words, by their very nature, fall into the shadow of their facetted parts; by their very agreements, undergo eclipse.

the breath catching on its own viscosity.

sublunar, subliminal, nothing's written, in effect, that's not underwritten: no world, in effect, that's not —ultimately— underworld.

within which —dense nexus— alluded.

having gutted the heart of every humor but its strange, abstract effulgence: its counter-trope.

whereby, on certain days, certain creatures, beautiful in the bulk of their luminous particles: in so much pure, undifferentiated mass.

whereby less, ever lesser, as it flexes with magnitude.

stripped, finally, of all gods, scriptures, all myth but the living mineral of the eyes as they vanish, now, beneath the roll of their own lashes.

whereby the word: the word-wordless: what would enter, now, the sheer immediacy of the remote.

wedging, as it did, that vaporous expanse: what had been, until then, meticulously withheld.

. . . the null, at last, as if invested . . .

in the rhyme of those matched annunciates, rendered palpable.

. . . there, just there, where the
mouth rounds to
its
scuttled rose, even the silence,
suddenly, would have
grown

re-
verberant.

PASTORAL

. . . was the way the fingers lay limp, supine,
over the coils of that
pillowed
bone. pastoral, a
plate glazed in the high flame of the

hal-
lucinatory. what's
there, quite suddenly, isn't: doors, windows,
furnishings, no, no more than the
night in the dim

floating cabochon of
its

stars. through the
least
whispers, now, would rise, gaze as the
languorous mirror
grew turgid. for it's that, that vitreous clay
you'd prod, moulding as you did the slick
facets of

fixation. here, but only
for that

feigned perdition, that mock
succumbing. here against the abeyant immensity of
no-
where, yes,
no-
where's once again, would
follow the line of a single finger as the finger it-
self —indolent prop— teased you past the
bulk of your

very
viscera. hump of

flowers on the
far
side of all history: yes, here, here's the hills and
here, the body's

lost botany. breathe it. yes, breathe that
red-
olent portrait before the
portrait it-
self
gets hissed into the hard shower of so
                                        many constituent cells.

FUGUES: ALL NIGHT THE NEOLITHIC

all night the neolithic
as if blew through your dreams: in long,
heron-bone hairpins, nestled in that thicket
that's no one's hair, no
one's odors, but the cellulated night's
dense honey.

---

already, the poem, basking in
its idol of syllables, exists in a
future you'd never, otherwise, have
known. yes, you who wrote it, read it, now, in the
very midst of an instant that's endlessly
drawing itself under.

---

there where a ladder
lay propped against the brittle, winter boughs, you'd
murmur the planets, wouldn't you, hiss
'saturn' as you lobbed the tangled, the
extraneous, brought your knuckles
eye-level with each, freshly pruned branch.

---

already, your new desk's
piled high with books, articles: you
who'd pillage history for its
lost dicta, abolished alphabets, for a
door left open, occasionally, on so much
thin, fibrous draft.

---

eliminated image but only, each
morning, for its
fresh scaffolds, hair streaming metallic
from the forehead backwards, catching on the
bars, struts, cross-pieces of so much sheer
evanescence.

---

worshipped only
what you'd failed to obliterate, efface in so
many rhythmic layers from the
glassy plates of the hallucinatory, oh
limb working limbs in a
shimmering thicket of whispers.

OF AIR AUGMENTED

. . . was air rushing through air that, each
time, solidified sound,
freckled the
still-

seething shadows with
sign, signature, the very stigmata, you'd
called them, of
semblance it-

self. would swell, wouldn't you, to those
sudden

complicities; watch the rocks as if knot on
so
many successive
conjugates. here, where fingers, whole

hearts get blown into the animate, an entire
landscape, this
very

instant, settles (orchard,
windbreak and battlement) within the
singular
respiration of its

disparate parts. here's only
here, you'd

written, in the ganging of its particles, in a
sudden
gust of the meticulously ar-

ticulated.

THE BODY BEING POROUS

the body being porous, spoke of
light as
solid, as a
density quilled on
whisper alone. pilgrim lost in
a

liturgy of
pebbles, it's the bees, now, that
magnify the

edifice. tell no one that the
mouth, the
deep crest of its wave, has come to

rest, finally, a-
gainst the
conch's

cracked pelvis.

TRANSPARENT ITINERARIES: 1994

. . . down through the
collapsed cubes
of
perspective, the page, at
last, encounters its own annunciates, begins sipping
at its

very letters, slaking on the
coil, dash, ellipsis of
its least, jotted
in-
scription.

---

for language, as you'd learnt, was never more than the arbitrary imprint of a violated silence.

the palace itself never more than the distant echo —the vestige, scarcely legible— of that original infraction.

—that sonorous usurpation—

'loanwords,' the paleolinguists called them. were there, indeed, any others, you asked yourself? had you ever known —employed— anything but?

crammed, as we are, syntactical: held to the absolutes of each, linguistic *monopole*, here —yes, here— in the midst of so much cryptic omission.

at the very heart, that is, of this elaborate mirage.

—this riddled script—

"Les Baroques savent bien que ce n'est pas l'hallucination qui feint la présence, c'est la présence qui est hallucinatoire." (Deleuze)

(ever, as you'd noted, a word away).

down the long corridor of your poems, though, would catch glimpses, wouldn't you?

there, for instance, where wisteria hung —weightless as rain— from its rusting trellises, would measure, as you gazed, the immensity of those locked receptacles.

enter —for whole moments at a time— their given intervals.

---

was 'something,' you'd
    written, and it's
nothing. was what the gold domes floating had
with-
held, capped in
their groined vaults. what's
less, far less than anything language

had ever
al-
lotted.

---

for wasn't the visible —after all— our *own* invention?

landscape but the shifting screens (the rocks, waterfalls, shrubbery) we'd deliberately slid over that archaic abyss?

all, as Focillon had put it, but a "quarrel of images"?

---

what draws us towards, however,
    would draw us through: yes, the sense, *senso*, of
anemones in their
fluffy

white corollas, the flesh it-
self as
if wrapt in the
taut knot of its own teased re-

leases.

---

for locked, the bodies travel backwards, root in the vast expanses —the lacunae— of their shuttered lids.

(buoyed by the euphoric particles of each, successive dispersion).

'a person,' as you'd written, 'named *persona*.'

a nobody, throning in the very midst of her own flushed abundance.

(what the mirrors would covet for themselves).

no 'here,' you realized, without the wind-ballast of some posited 'there.'

without the warranty of some richly invested naught.

". . . drew us, thanks to its veil, all the closer." (Benjamin on *aura*).

as you, living already in the resonance of an absentee's pronoun, made these deposits in the very midst of so much erasure.

. . . lay them, leaded
with breath, a-
gainst
their

vaporous tabernacles.

THE ARCHEOLOGIST: A BROKEN DICTATION

(la Grotte de l'Escale)

. . . had never been further, you'd
told us; never before
taken the
full measure of 'origins,' you'd
said (your words, already, tattering in mid-

air; reaching us, now, only in so
much

semantic particle. 'glacier,' for instance,
then, weeks
later, something
about roses. 'roses,' you'd said, as
if, having ventured —yes, already— into an
aftermath of

roses, only the utterance, now, as if
subsisted, and even
that, only in splinters —yes, these

brief,
intermittent sparks).

~

itinerary, then, if,
indeed, there were one; if, that
is, one
might have assumed
some kind of sequence, unravelling, other than
that, say, the

fates played, ineluctable. would
sleep, wouldn't you, your
eyes

opened wide on a world without shadows. there,
where doors never closed, had
counted hearths, hadn't
you, those charred,
paper-

thin deposits in which, you'd
tell us, they —yes, they, the very first— first
cupped, incredulous, the
un-

touchable.

~

'cinder,' you'd reported, and,
sometime later,
'psalm.' of you, though, squatting
a-
mongst your
plumb lines, sunlight
shimmering down the blade of your scalpel, knew, in

fact, nothing. knew, for all
our
overloaded circuitry, only
this growing paucity, rarefaction, the lapses that
lay, now, be-

tween one substantive
and an-
other. whole weeks, for

instance, between 'ash,' say, and 'ochre,' the
words themselves as if
wafted, now, on
ever-

more
tenuous
frequencies. of you, though, of

you sifting
through so much sediment for some
all-
determinate, all-
establishing, evolutionary instant, no,

nearly nothing, now, if
not, yes, 'roses' sometimes, and

sometimes 'wind.' 'twinge,' too, as if some
minor, recurrent, muscular
contraction (a
memento of
sorts) still held you, there in the midst of
all

that stratified
calcination.

                    no, had never been further, you'd
told us, never before
come to
measure, as they'd called it, so much
'eloquent vestige.' yes, there, just there, as

your words scattered in the
very
updrafts wherein
words first had, as if hesitatingly, a-

risen.

II

Late Bronze, Early Iron: A Journey Book

LATE BRONZE, EARLY IRON: A JOURNEY BOOK

once again, found yourself travelling in the direction of your own broken landscapes.

plumbing sound, extracting fracture.

there where the air —either side— had gone saline.

'glasswort,' you'd jotted down as if the word alone, in those blanched expanses, might outlast—even for an instant—the very marsh plant it designated.

gulls, egrets, now, in growing numbers.

while, far out, stands of maritime pine as if floated —mirage-like— in bunched clusters.

felt yourself, as you went, thin to that spread estuary.

its last, scattered shacks: penultimate markers.

'a traced erasure,' you'd once called it. a semiotics, finally, without signs.

as the road, just under, broke, now, into gravel, rubble, dune.

impression, everywhere, of aftermath: of having entered, already, an afterworld; of muttering to yourself in some kind of after-language.

you, who'd chase yourself down, if you could, to your least, legible vestige.

entering, as you went, those abolished alphabets.

just there, for instance, where they'd located —along the tidal limits— traces of that protohistoric conglomerate: mounds (*taparas*) emanating out of so much vanished habitat.

'pudding stone,' they'd called it.

or on tiny, offshore islands, the first, readily identifiable potsherds of that incinerating culture: the urnfield.

wondered, didn't you, why the faintest residues elicited the strongest responses? the most resonant?

delving, as you did, for echo.

for the parallel register(s) of some possible accompaniment.

where, within so much sounding —precise, punctual— might have coincided (even for an instant) with that *terro sutile.*

(as the ground, otherwise, went on slipping from under).

mattered, didn't it, that —in approaching the coastline— the very same, incised ceramic had gone from a clay tempered in quartz, calcite, feldspar to one of crushed, glistening seashell.

—earth and artifact, so doing, in perfect symbiosis—

against those innate dispositions, would read —as you went— your own, makeshift arrangements.

matching —as you did— precarities.

moving, now, no longer as a physical entity but so much scribble, scratch-mark, pecking.

as a broken phrase in search of its own complement.

words, now, nothing more than the solvent for other words: a breath-tracking-breath across so much spectral landscape.

so many long-since fossilized sites.

even (in the rhetoric of latter-day archeology) 'fossilized waters.'

there where the *terramaricoles* had settled at the mouth of the least creek, rivulet, watercourse.

mattered, too, that the lowest stratigraphic layer of human habitation could be determined, today, by whether or not the bivalves therein (cockles, mussels, clams, etc.) still *happened to be hinged.*

or, occasionally, by an urn, still choked with crematory ash.

would, if you could, precede vestige.

reach, that is, far enough back that you might begin, finally, projecting forwards.

bearing —as you did— that open vocable.

as you travelled, now, well past the silence of those abandoned settlements (sacrificed, no doubt, circa -550, for the sake of the first, fortified cities to the west).

rendered derelict by an emergent, mercantile exchange system, undermining every form of autonomous economy.

as you entered, just then, the *cami salinié*—the ancient salt route— leading past the last, lagoonal outposts.

—visor lowered against so many flat, oncoming rays—

would, if you could, precede even the instant itself; by only a syllable, only the living increment of a murmur.

(prolonged draft of one's own inaudibility).

as, either side, the vinerows went on ticking (dark, invisible now) past the cracks in the car's windows.

usually stopped, didn't you, at one of those small, one-star hotels along the outskirts as if the choice of place depended —as with the word itself— on its very liminality.

for dinner, fried squid and a dry, white Minervois. moved, as you went, at the exact same rhythm as whatever you'd assimilated.

within the rented space of that tiled bedroom (windowdoors the same height as the room itself), sheer length of that fractured reflection.

what wrapped, just now, about its very husk.

throughout the night, the occasional shouts, just beneath, of passing bargemen.

echoing —syncretic— against the running silence of so much antecedent.

travelling, as they did, down the long, ruler-straight corridor of that antique canal: what lay, just now, beneath a high, overhanging canopy of dry, unrattling plane leaves.

where, only five kilometers lower, a Gallo-Roman epigraph had been found dedicated to the god Mars by the shipwrights of that very locality.

the inscription thereof, DEO. MARTI. AVG., leading, as it would, to the discovery of Lattara: city lost —choked— in the alluvium of the very watercourse it once abutted.

(what if you yourself came across the word —the words— by which you, too, might be decrypted?)

(could roam, pseudo-antiquarian, amongst so much interpolated vestige?)

"pity," as one archeologist put it, "that the site itself hadn't been ravaged by fire: the calcination that would have resulted might have preserved many of its artifacts from so much needless deterioration."

enough remained, nonetheless, within its hydromorphic subsoils, to distinguish eleven separate levels of habitation.

(at its very deepest, for instance, abundant evidence of *bucchero nero*, Etruscan blackware).

enough remained, that is, to determine the fact that Lattara had not only overpowered those scattered, lagoonal settlements but come to monopolize the entire territory in an embryonic attempt at colonization: at establishing, already, an oligarchic microstate.

characterized —most notably— by a "flourishing of ramparts."

by the first appearance, *intra muros*, of granaries: evidence, already, of a surplus production and its automatic corollary: the stocking of exchangeable merchandise.

yes, already, concepts of deferral.

just as the phrase, that most invested of goods, would come to gather, provisionally, against its own diffusion.

clot, thesaural.

no way of evaluating the true worth of 'here,' you realized, without a thoroughgoing examination of its historical determinants.

without, for instance, measuring (as had the archeologists) the vast quantities of gravel, of paving stone the founders had first employed in consolidating the 'here' —for example— of this particular site.

(what would only add, centuries later, to its subsidence. like Ostia, its vanishing).

yes, here, just here, where horses, this morning, grazed immobile amongst the excavated substructures.

—that skeletal, pluricellular network of rectangles—

(punctuated, occasionally, by black cypress).

were you, you wondered, any more substantial than the reflections you cast against the glass cases in the adjoining museum, stocked with so much tagged salvage?

than that wafer-thin layer, glazing the surface of so many illegibles?

yes, would delve: delve if you could.

among the toponyms (those earliest, verbal particles), would follow the radical *Lat-*, signifying —in Celt— a bog or swampland as far as its suffix *-ara, -aris,* designating —in a lost, pre-Indo-European dialect— water, running water.

ur-words, of sorts. *urspracht.*

those, that is, of an entire world —worlds— gone under: there, just there, as you stood at the fixed center of so much latter-day postulate.

so many vaporous substantives.

the rub of your own coat collar serving, occasionally, as reminder.

—or the jingle, just then, of your car keys—

fragrance, as you passed, of so many damp, rotting birch leaves.

as you took, now, the river valley northwards, retracing, as you did, the route (and, subsequently, the dialectic) which once existed between the protohistoric settlements along the coast (e.g., Lattara, Agatha, etc.) and the rich hinterlands, above.

between negotiant, that is, and producer.

following, no doubt, that "axis of penetration" which the first, itinerant bronzesmiths must have taken, vectors —initiators— of the new order.

rising, as you went, towards those abandoned *oppida* perched on their rock outcrops.

Ensérune, Montlaurès, La Monadière.

(only visible, at that time of year, through a blizzard of amber, salmon, brass).

as a narrow footpath —taut with aleppo— as if drafted you upwards.

where, once again, you'd find them: the substructures. again and again, the human signature of so much right angle lying at the base of so many obliterated dwellings.

while the earth, a bit everywhere, oozed vestige.

oozed *dolia*.

unmistakable, the fragments of those immense, subterranean storage jars as they began appearing —a bit everywhere, now— in broad, scarcely baked, convex sections.

the very length, quite often, of a human collarbone.

shards that the archeologists had come to associate, chronologically, with the emergence of the earliest known battlements, watch towers, defense systems.

yes, once again, that "flourishing of ramparts."

at the very same moment, in fact, as the fortified cities along the coast: these sudden, rudimentary hill citadels.

at the dawn, that is, of a market economy (i.e., the aforementioned production of an agrarian surplus and its subsequent conservation as a negotiable), these massive circumscriptions.

communities that —already— had begun gathering *against.*

as you, in a science of your own, would trace, if you could, the envelopment of the verb —of language itself— in a similar set of constrictions. self-enclosures.

how, against the innate radiance (call it *aura*) of a polymorphous diffusion, language —as well— would undergo a near identical circumscription.

find itself slowly, inexorably locked within the fixed perimeters of the literal.

(breath itself as if monetized).

yes, a process, a linguistic degeneration, you realized, long in coming: in the gradual attrition of so many sonorous particles.

for ‘here’ was never more than what a ‘there’ initiated.

than the ever-narrowing values placed upon language itself: an instrument, today, reduced to the inventorial. for each, specific item, nothing more —now— than its quick, correspondent code.

nothing more —in the spoliation of each, earthly good— than so much successive, electronic spasm.

had thinned as it went, hadn’t it?

as you’d entered the very heart, now, of the cumulative, had nearly vanished —you realized— altogether.

you who’d sift substance —if you could— for sound. read, in the eloquence of so much rubble, in the cracked, terracotta skulls of so much vestige, traces of those lost vocables.

institute, in sort, an archeology of the transitive.

for you’d always assumed, as you went, an *âge d’or.* as nothing more, perhaps, than some psychic imperative: an underworld, still bristling with signifiers.

yes, would delve: annotate each, discrete breath-particle.

just as others would measure, as they had, annual rainfall in the very midst of the Bronze Age.

calculate —down to the last millimeter— the otherwise obliterated.

unearthing (here at the Cayla de Mailhac, for instance) evidence of a virtually autonomous, self-sustaining culture, a "unity of civilization," as they'd called it, anteceding that of the first, surplus-oriented market economies, a century later.

towards the very end, that is, of the ephemeral urnfields (870–700 B.C.).

bronze, already, edging towards iron.

where, in their excavations, they'd discovered no dwelling larger than another; no sepulcher, richer.

a people who'd existed, no doubt, in the immensity of the immediate: in the very *there* of 'there.'

without a politic, that is, of deferral, of speculation against the eventual: a people who'd existed, no doubt, in the very glow of their own voices.

for the phrase only fails in failing to generate.

only fails in failing to distribute, *ipso facto,* its own, sonorous properties.

(radial, self-absolving).

there, just then, where another people —a warrior people— would arrive, now, bearing iron.

bearing the clanging axeheads of the new order.

and, from one year to the next (700 B.C.), the lovely, coiled, Mailhacian ceramic —incised, as it was, with a whole proto-alphabet of paired, echoing pictographs— would find itself replaced by that, now, of the thumb-slash.

by *those* of the thumb-slash.

and, along with them, the immediate hierarchization of social structures, the complexification of labor, and —inevitably—the sudden, spectacular emergence of market economies.

'almost ourselves,' you might have whispered, moving, just then, through the tall grasses, the grasses themselves still ticking with the very last crickets of autumn.

'almost ourselves,' you might have heard, reverberant.

a bit everywhere, now, screens, pails, the scuttled equipment of so much long-since abandoned excavation.

(turning, already, to vestige itself).

as you, existing as you did only an instant —a diaphanous moment— ahead of your own occlusion, made your way, now, through the narrow passage of so much sporadic murmur.

under, you'd insisted, but only for the sake of *through*.

only for the sake of resuscitating a language light, impalpable, diffuse as death itself.

one's very cells, therein, rendered weightless.

one's very breath —at last— as if ballasted in air.

while you stood there, that very instant, watching the sun —deep persimmon— set over the gutted necropolis.

and felt, so doing, the infallible contraction.

—the knot, knotting—

were there, you wondered, rooms, corridors, lobbies spacious enough to contain the immensity of so much empty speculation?

mirrors set at angles sufficiently congruous to catch the dark drafts of those vaporous reflections?

for the invisible —you knew— had all but vanished.

(gone, down the tall columns, unquoted).

you, who'd only written for the *wasn't,* only gutted the syllables for the sake of a certain *nothing*, moved now —as if impacted— within the mask of so much organ, nerve-end.

(so many self-replicating qualifiers).

catching glimpses, in the rearview, of that very self as you flicked, now, through the narrow, squat, stucco-fronted towns of the Minervois.

(felt, each time, the jolt of their tiny, humpbacked bridges).

Aigues-Vives, Cabezac, St. Marcel-sur-Aude.

travelling fast, now, beneath the vaulted ceilings of the sycamores: their leaves, in the flooded yellow of your headlights, twice gold.

leaves, trees, the *richly irrigated plains* now of the Aude valley: wasn't the breath itself for burning?

these very words —on that vaporous altar— for offering?

wasn't it thus, indeed, that we'd always proceeded? yielding unto nothing, nothing again?

but the meats, you specified. but the chosen meats of our murmurs —you insisted— for the sake of passage.

passage alone.

as you crossed, just then —planks rattling— the Canal de Robine.

(its waters skeined in the night's first fog).

and saw, only moments later, Narbonne as if floating —lavishly lit— over its dark, parcelled orchards.

—what you'd enter, now, ever initiate—

a dense concentration, in fact, of avenues, esplanades, restaurants, their windows wrapt in ovals of blue neon.

your hotel bedroom itself like some station in space.

NARBO MARTIUS, you'd read.

in letters long as your own forearm and chiselled three centimeters deep in limestone: yes, these, even these, to be blown —so many open vocables— as if across.

yes, unto nothing, no one's, once again, *sleeve, wrist, fingers,* as if offered.

this very text, indeed, for its own unmaking.

for 'wasn't it thus,' as you'd written, 'we'd always proceeded?' in nourishing that very vacuum, subsisted?

charged —as we are— by our own releases?

yes, even here, where nothing happens, happens —indeed— over and over.

wind, that very instant, catching in the loose muslins.

the whole room, in fact, swelling with air.

as you stood, now, in the very space that your phrase —only an instant earlier— had vacated.

while the waxed floortiles, before you, glistened.

III

Substantia Separata

ACCORDING TO SENECA

. . . every wind, according to
Seneca, has
its
origins in some deep-
seated stellar configuration. once, every
word, its every

blown
vocable, came rippling out of an else-

where that
was. edge, then, towards what? you, who'd
scraped pebbles, goaded
shadows, hover,
now, in the

coves of imploded
al-

lusion. here, where even the air, this
morning, lies as if
im-
pacted, yes, in so
many exhausted particles, would

feed yourself, wouldn't you, to
the
slightest interstice, oversight, pry free of
your own, in-
exorable

replication. for just beyond would lie the
bars,
chords, the

sonorous reefs of
some suggested passage. whisper, then. yes,

murmur the
wavering blue line of that
taut,
tenuous horizon: 'wind,' 'waves,' whitecaps,'
what, in

themselves, meant nothing, whereas nothing, you
knew, without them (burst,
pulverized) could
possibly
mean.

FUGUES: THERE'S ONLY 'THERE'

there's only 'there,' you
wrote, *withheld.* you who'd enter that
very withholding, exchanging
what you were for something you'd never
even imagined, gaze now at that
countenance, caught in the interface of
its already dissolving reflections.

---

vaporous, the heart's
sharpest crystals, our most vehement points
of fixation. wash of
glances, sheath of muscles: you, moving already
amongst the crushed syllables, no longer, now,
even the unequivocal 'neither's.'

---

with the air, this morning, smelling of
iron, marvelled at the buds too tiny, the
lacquered horns of the
burgeoning cherries too
slight, for any sound but your breath's
measured omissions.

---

already, the first dragonflies
track backwards: is the air's
undertow and the heart's that
takes us, each time, under: oh cell weaving
cells on the loom of a once
unassailable imperative.

(La Musée d'Arles Antique)

would wash, wouldn't you, before visiting
those water-slick marble torsos: the
scattered segments of that long-
since abolished mirror. oh eyes in the
orbit of eyes, tell us to ourselves before the
telling dissipates, fades, undergoes
dismemberment itself.

---

there, the windier it grows, the
lusher. what with the irises clanging mute, had
brought yourself level
with that tenuous band of
pure translucence (nothing you'd write
that you couldn't breathe; that breathing,
gaze through).

---

would finally return, wouldn't you,
to your own pronoun, but only
through the
richly ploughed sonorities of the poem, the
prototext itself, devoid now
of all authorship whatsoever.

RÉPLIQUE: AN ARS POETICA

gnawed at drafts, at the
    least oversight in the air's otherwise
air-
tight vacuum. bubbles, too,

'bubbles,' you'd
re-

iterated, as your mouth came to
crater an
antique particle that not even you, now,
could

interpolate. slake, then, on
what? on so many
stray

tumescent beads? had we
reached, finally reached, then, com-

pletion at last? already entered the in-
violate ring of some
pure,
perfectly in-

exhaustible series of self-
rep-
lications?

                nomina nuda, what "can be
used
as though never
previously proposed." what can be uttered
with-
out any substantive other than one's own

pulsate insistence. like a shrub budding,
you'd called it, at the
skull's

very base, but not. like a
breeze, too, catching at the very tip of its
breeze-
roots, but not. you who'd brought
the

podded cells of your sounds beating
a-

gainst nothing, really, but the hollow body
of light alone, had written these words
as
witness to the

poem's very presence, syllables
slapping against the
shanks of some
thin,

still evanescent
réplique.

CONTRAPUNTAL

slept in your
own
shifting imprint, breath-
deep over so many successive layers of

crushed artefact. ankle, flank, shoulder:
weren't these, after
all, attributes of

air, what you'd wager a-
gainst your own unmaking? but wrought,
beaten, first, into

bright scales; the least bones buoyant
with

number.

                              would lie, then, in
long waves of
sound, knuckles as
if wafted, each organ inscribed
within its own

tenuous register. a world-without, you'd
called it, hovering
a-

bout its
very
obliteration. ash and amber, jug and

tegulae: what drew, would draw incessant from
under, while your
fist
clenched, milky, the

resonant
cloud.

FASTIA

"inane fulmen fabae . . ."

under the sun's high
  pewter-white halo, your breath went
even lighter, your
body a

mere incident in the
mediation of its parts. a *there,* then, but
only in its

blown
configurants as,
sacrificial, in Ovid's
Fastia, the bean sprouts, stripped of
all

but their
desiccated stalks. no, nothing's too slight if,

unbound, unwritten,
un-
ascribable, the
nul having entered, *in silentio*, the
vacated passage, the lips might feed, avid, on their own

gutted
succulents.

SPIRITUS ASPER

everything's allegory but the fibrous text in the very instant of its own unravelling.

but the breath's relentless dismemberments.

society itself allegorical: the instruments of its domination never more than a more or less generalized agreement to *actualize* such allegory.

(legitimize one given variant over another).

while with each, successive violation, had felt ourselves as if emptied into an ever-gathering enormity.

de-defined; de-defining.

with nothing, now, but the threads —the trailer phrases— of so much late annunciate.

but the slapping of their tattered pennants.

there where the bodies —feigning embodiment— had worked, teased, as if insinuated themselves through the narrow corridors of the whereless.

the organs —alone— swollen like trophies.

was something, we'd written, and it's nothing. *something,* kept insisting, as if the words —in their irrepressible releases— might be eviscerated enough to warrant reception.

might, in the draft of some consummately hollowed phrase, actually accede.

"actually accede" as it reverberates, now, down the successive ranks of its own echoes.

and, as it fades, penetrates.

(just there, where the wind had glazed its puffed cirrus nacreous).

the hypothetical landscapes of the conditional having become, finally, our last, viable ground.

the tenuous fields of some eventual identity.

because it's never *here* that it happened. never *here,* but in the air's empty resonance (was what the bodies —locked, vaulted— hesitated before, as if held in the imminence of their own undoing).

our breath alone translative.

~

oh room in the
oblit-
eration of
rooms, in the abolished rhetoric of

fixture, it's there, in
those
witnessing cells we'd
thrive, drawing —from its
deepest mirrors— that glitter, that

thick,
im-
petuous milk.

TOWARDS THE BLANCHED ALPHABETS

. . . like so much weather
out of the west, sound arrives with its
scooped
hollows, the caves it makes in the
very midst of

mass. wrapped, now, in the
blanched
half

of antiphon, you're carried in its
quick, irresonant folds, its
mute
répliques. saying only
what you can't, haunting only
what isn't, you drift, now, through the

intervals. there, in those
late
landscapes, that
vaporous ground: grammar's

ultimate retreat. really yours, these
fingers? this breath
dismembered
for the sake of some final reprieve?
spoke, you

wrote, where speech couldn't, spelling
'hand' free
from hand, 'moon'

from its florid marshes. were
what's left, the
air's
least outlines: mask
that's creasing the folds of the face, there,

just there, where the face
had
already vanished.

CHASSELAS

glottal, these jades rot
in the damp
autumn
air. this far, then, and

no further? had the
message meant that
there's

none? the code but
sheathing
for a

gutted husk? sleep, then,
in

fingers, the podded outlines
of ought. only there,
under the

pressed weight
of
lashes, would the
swollen word, at last, burst

open.

PSEUDO-SEMANTIC

. . . in long drafts, the shadows, the
viscera's, wrap to
a
mouth; bunch but only

for their own
ob-

literation. raft
of
whispers, elisions, dis-
seminations: you, who'd murmured of
mass, spoke, in

fact, of
solvents. yes, there, where the
room
had drifted from under, the breath but

smoke and
crystals, relinquished the
coils, the
curls, the hard air that held you fixated to all
that

arbitrary
ideation.

TRANSPARENT ITINERARIES: 1995

you who'd fallen through your own body, measured clouds, now, the buoyancy of certain masses.

amongst the flaked paints of the wind, read fortunes.

---

skimming the very surface of the in-
    determinate, hands
without fingers, fingers with-
out words, words without any further consistency
than the

lacquer that a gaze once
laid a-
cross so many seeming

in-
effaceables.

---

only rhythmic, in lyric increments, would you enter, now, the obliterated.

—as a witness of sorts to the inexistent—

who'd imagined yourself, occasionally, as some kind of baroque day-laborer, scaffolding voids.

res nullius: on no one's grounds.

there, over the shorn wheatfields, where the sun, it seemed, wouldn't stop setting.

oh *aura*, angel of phenomenology and ultimate guardian, as such, of those dissolved margins.

---

having arrived, at long last, on that terrace
of smoking chimneypots, nothing
lay before you, now, but the flight
of your very eyes, but the
clouds, but the broken pages
of so many broken clouds.

". . . the pain of melancholia," wrote Freud, "is due to the dissolving of . . . associations."

there where the verb, once, had lain muscled within the reverberant.

each breath the brittle rose, once, of its own response.

shard, then, if shard speaks.

if, in an end-world, an end-object continues to emit, as if by inadvertence, the ghostly particles of some otherwise arrested sequence.

(propagating, you well realized, a grammar of its own).

an inclination towards . . .

'towards what?' would cry out the hordes of the long-since eviscerated.

---

screen rippling on the
far, the
facing, the gaze-
impacted surface of so much cellular
im-

perative, 'you,' you'd
said, 'unto you, you who'd

come, suddenly, into
such
im-

maculate focus.'

---

are but only to the extent you'd enter that *isn't.*

shedding, as you went, each and every instance of the allusive.

every other 'other' but that.

while the mouth went round —agape— with its own open vocable.

what, in turn, silent as it was imperious, world transit.

BLUE, SHE SAID

. . . would vanish
within those accomplished spaces: you, who'd
lived on
el-

lipsis alone, on the intermittent heart of
your
own coiled viscera. blue, you'd
ask. blue, keep insisting.
blue a-

mongst the
cleaved waves of those meticulously
executed mountains. doesn't the foam, at last,

catch fire? you who'd enter, finally, that
very insertion, slipping past
the

pounding of so much
swollen
mirror, edge emptiness, now, with these broken
tokens. beyond you, not even the

wind-
tufted grasses
weather their dark idyll.

FLORA

. . . was all
about opening, you wrote, the
breath-cells
bursting vacuous in the very
midst of

that abundant
convolvulation, the no-grail, at

last, lodged in the deep
froth of
so
much seething, evanescent foliage.

THE GUITARIST: A CELEBRATION IN GREY

for Robert Creeley

grey heat, grey
    hunger, you'd elaborated on grey's each
individual variant, here in the
hills where the least
hollow

puddles a grey so
luminous you'd
mis-

taken it for what the wind, wind-
grey, had
slaked off the flat, hammered surface of the
waters. yes, here in
the

hills, where it no longer mattered, where
you'd abandoned the very
organs
of identity; had blown eyes, tongue, teeth
through the pinched eyelets of
that
wizened mask, mattered, didn't it, that

you'd brought the notes, note-
grey, to

wobble, at last, in
their
shallow
sockets. yes, here on the far, on the
facing, the

antipodal side, had given the heart, hadn't
you, counter-
parts

~

grey, then, in a rainbow of
greys, in an
un-

ending variation upon the virtually
un-
variable, was nothing 'here,' you wrote, that
wasn't 'there,' but

bleached, tempered, brought sonorous, finally,
to bear. yes, blue as grey
ever
gets, even the air, finally, arranged, abey-

ant, something
you'd
no longer breathe, now, on the
burning stick of some self-extinguishing breath,
but

modulate, innovate,
play.

~

caves,
con-
cavities, the sumptuous shelters of the exclusively
acoustic, there's an

exact
volume to
angst; another to the
floating, unresolved outlines of every incipient
ex-

hilaration. oaks, green
as
grey ever gets, grey-viridian in a field of
flickering
grey poppies, you've entered a

world, now, which
isn't. you, already, amongst
the
resonant bars of mint, sawtooth, coriander,
nothing more, now,
than

these nacreous ledges that you've set
your-
self to; than this
hand, flushed as grey

ever gets, plucking gold, grey gold, a pale,
transparent, hand-hammered
gold, gold as
grey

ever gets across the pounded board, now, of the
thoroughly ac-
corded.

IV

Reading Sarcophagi: An Essay

for Jolaine

Si come ad Arli, ove Rodana stagna . . .
Dante, *Inferno* IX:112

READING SARCOPHAGI: AN ESSAY

of air, once, analogous.

of an age in which all things, once, in counterpoint, thrived echoic, reflexive: in which image substantiated substance.

—each organ keyed to that of its own remote anatomy—

(in running sequences, that infallible parallel).

yes, even here, among these gutted cisterns: here, where the dead, once, lay enveloped in narrative, in episodes hewn, chiseled, rasped out of so much white, luminescent marble.

their corpses as if incorporated.

within a solid fume, say, of branches, apples, doves, as if transliterated.

one scenic program after another depicting (no matter how mythologic the subject) some aspect of life prolonged, perpetuated: the limbs, here, having no other referent than limbs.

(the muscles but their plump, recumbent muscles).

beginning, as you had, with Hadrian's revival of corporal inhumation; yes, here, within this rich, decorous milieu, you'd noted, annotated, hadn't you? measured as you went.

cataloging, as you did, the discrete panels of a world whose original semiotic intent had all but vanished.

you who'd arrived late, too late, in these long, empty corridors to acknowledge anything more than the aesthetic prowess (*technē*) involved in so much scuttled ontology.

the profound gouging, for instance, which allowed the figures in those earliest Greco-Roman sarcophagi to stand out in such bold, contoured relief.

the goddess Aura, for example, detached, autonomous, ebullient in the rippling chiaroscuro of her own figuration.

the least tendon, ligament, chiseled free of its underlying sepulchral mass.

to enter, finally, pure similitude.

"In formal terms, the hollowing out of volumes and their arrangement in superimposed planes suggest a tridimensional space corresponding to a visible reality: humankind in a world made to its own measure."[1]

yes, the limbs, here, having no other referent than limbs.

panel after panel, secular and sacred coexisting in an interplay of reciprocal signifiers.

in the fragile status, that is, of the uninterrupted.

so that the souls of the dead, blown by so many winged masks, might alight, finally, as if on the far side of the very same mirror, wearing the exact same sandals, tunics and accessories, celebrating, thus, their perfect convertibility.

weren't these, in fact, the very landscapes you'd traced, recorded? that world in default of worlds you'd gone on exploring?

reduced as you were to so much scenography?

scarcely noticing, as you went, in the midst of all that late pagan signature (tritons, centaurs, wood nymphs, the mythic figure of Night, her arms filled with long stalks of poppy), the first, cryptic insignias of the new faith.

works commissioned, in fact, by a class of rich, recently converted landowners, still languishing in the long, bucolic twilight of Antiquity.

wherein, for instance, naked amoretti would be depicted plucking olives from an olive orchard whose leaves came to camouflage a single, diminutive, all-but-invisible cruciform.

or, on either side of a medallion in which an evangelized couple stood portrayed, the Dioscuri still serving as psychopomps.

went on reading those panels, didn't you, tracing in chronological order their evolving eschatology.

that unending succession of hallucinatory responses to so much blunt, obdurate history.

you yourself little more, in fact, than history's fugitive, seeking in all that image —that dense iconography— some inexistent exit.

reading each episode as a potential door, an hermetic passageway.

discovering, now, the very first scenes drawn, unabashedly, from scripture: yes, the invocation, already, of the guileless, miraculous, remote.

(what followed, no doubt, immediately upon Constantine's conversion, 312 A.D.).

Noah, for example, delivered from the flood or Moses, leading his people, charismatic, over the waters.

each, as you'd noted, a celebration of passage, coming as it had (out of the furthest reaches eastward) with the emergence of mystery cults: the awakening of mysteries.

of what has been called "the secret self."

unto what promised lands, though, you'd asked yourself? what epiphanies?

the strigillated wave-pattern whipped sinuous towards whose "blessed isles"?

for clearly the visible had shifted ground, given way, camped now in the diminishing perspective of a growing enigma.

as the gaze, yes, the beautiful gaze of those enlightened figures turned inwards, mused increasingly, now, on the inscrutable.

(while, without, the Empire went on crumbling).

(its frontiers —what had once delineated a rich mythopoetics of its own— went on diminishing).

under, went under.

only closed, now, would the lids envelop light.

the sarcophagi themselves, by now, no longer extolling a life bucolic, self-perpetuating but, by suggestion —implication— indicating something altogether *other.*

buoyed by the rumor, yes, by the all-glowing radiance of so much promissory vision.

the "humble, now, replacing the superb," their figures rendered squat, thick-set, of equal stature, their robes as if bumping one against the other in tight, complicitous circles.

what you, pseudo-aesthete, went on measuring.

determining, as you did, an ever-increasing loss of relief between foreground and background: between, say, an apostle's right elbow in slight projection and his left shoulder, dissolving already into the anonymous magma.

as if those glistening, soap-smooth figures were being undermined from under; their own divine status, as if aspirated.

"Relation, by its very essence, isn't something in itself," wrote Thomas Aquinas, "but *tends* toward something."[2]

anagoge: from Greek, *an:* beyond; *agein:* to lead.

"beyond the literal, allegorical and moral senses a fourth and ultimate . . . sense."[3]

you, who would have lingered, if you could, among the palms, in so many scenes of manifest felicity —yes, in all that landscape of miracle— lingered, in fact, nowhere.

(was nowhere, finally, wherein you could).

(fixating, for instance, on some particular iconographic detail —the three magi, for example, a star blazing against each of their foreheads— in which you'd enjoy, even vicariously, some fleeting sense of refuge).

some albeit feigned impression of belonging.

held, as you were, to sequence, history's inexorable tug, could only appreciate those epiphanous moments in relation to the exact manner of their execution.

that and their evolving.

how, for instance, the figures lay increasingly outlined (undercut) in a futile attempt, now, to capture —against so many late rays of sunlight— the very last semblance of volume.

(as the episodes themselves grew more and more detached, disconnected, paratactic).

the stout colonnades that had once risen into so many thick, fruit-choked capitals, no more, now, than a faint, ephemeral decor, lacking any architectural coherence whatsoever.

as the Empire itself, already divided since Theodosius's death (395) between East and West, went on contracting from without, disintegrating from within.

Rome sacked; Provence laid low by Franks, Visigoths.

while the "somber speculations of the gnostics" expressed, with ever-growing fervor, a renunciation of the flesh and all images —representations— thereof.

a time, now, of "holy men," masters of jackals and lions.

of the *anachoresis*, signifying in Egyptian "the displaced:" a desert creature in rupture with the all-dominant ethos of the city, the Latin *civitas.*[4]

emerges, now, a world remote.

emerges a world "invisible, impalpable, incorporal, immeasurable."[5]

as essence comes to supercede appearance; sign, the signified.

wherein, for five centuries running, would vanish Daniel and his lions, Jacob and his ladder, the loaves and fishes lying plump at the very tip of a pointed finger.

all semblance, methodically eliminated.

would beckon angels, now, and seraphs, the messengers of that very ideation.

wherein "flesh" would find itself inexorably consumed by "word."

and "word" —soon enough— by its own inaudible whisper.

as a delicately carved pair of marble curtains, scintillating like so much compressed sugar, came unfolded upon a perfectly empty, perfectly deserted, stage-like decor.

"you heard a voice speaking, but saw no figure; there was only a voice." (*Deuteronomy*, 4:12).

was only, you'd add, the scuttled vessels of that voice, that foam, the seething particles of that disintegrated mirror.

aureoled, now, in an elsewhere.

a nowhere.

in giving its flesh and figure to the essence of withdrawal, that very invisibility takes possession of all worldly visibilities."[6]

no, you'd settled nowhere; was nowhere, now, in which to settle.

as the gaze, if anything, slid accelerating across those aniconic panels, mined as it was, now, to the uninterrupted.

"for five centuries running," a total absence of inscription, decor: of the least, convolvulated tendril.

the flanks of those coffins, now —spot-lit in the long, abandoned corridors you'd passed through— slick as water, anonymous as air.

(were what, already, foretold, prefigured us).

as you recorded —scribbled, really— this sequence into that crowded notebook of yours.

and saw, in paraphrase, your own words come unwritten.

Notes

[1] Jean-Pierre Caillet, Helmuth Nils Loose, *La Vie d'éternité*, Éditions du Cerf, Paris 1990

[2] Thomas Aquinas, *Summa Theologiqua* (Quod 1, ix, a4)

[3] Jean-Pierre Caillet, Helmuth Nils Loose, *ibid.*

[4] Peter Brown, *The World of Late Antiquity,* Thames & Hudson Ltd., London, 1971

[5] Jean-Pierre Caillet, Helmuth Nils Loose, *ibid.*

[6] Marie-José Mondzain, *Image, icône, économie,* Éditions du Seuil. Paris 1996

V

Like the Opening and Closing of Clouds

A WORLD OF LETTERS

. . . just where dawn broke
over its
scattered relics, you'd entered outline, the
vague schema of so much
a-

bandoned intent.   a 'world of letters,' they'd
once called it.   called it
phalanx and

metacarpal, the air that moved, that very
instant, against
its
grazed mirrors, the promise that
no one made, long since

re-
scinded.

NEVER MORE THAN NEITHER

for J.M.

only a breath denser than
air it-
self, would feed
on those shredded red petals: the very meats
of some self-

revelation. within, weren't the
hills, the
dust's driven particles, even sharper? even
more

prismatic? you who'd sleep in the
heap of your
own
hallucinations, molding as you did your own
weight against so

many idle
out-

lines, live in this
stasis, these islands, the irrefutable pages of
this in-

existent work. does it
dangle, does it glint —you ask— the
Medusa's
head, heavy in the mirrors your

mouth once drew
across so
much scuttled shadow? eat this, chew that.
nothing's

never more than
neither in the very instant
it
couples.

CRYPT

. . . would enter, over and over, that
very part with-
held, its
crypt

flourishing with image. nowhere's
too far, you knew, for that
spatial

contraction, there where your
breath, at
last, would scatter into
so

many chromatic
particles.

AURA, AUREOLE

. . . called it *aura*, *aureole*, what lay, like
rolled vapor, at the very
edge of the
air's
empty receptacle (what, in turn, you'd

fill with
objects, the jingling charms, say, of some
lost
monodic. whose hair, whose hands, whose
heart —yes, all
those

'heavenly props,' as you'd
called them— would swell, reverberant, to their
last, vacuous
ripple). for wasn't it thus, in

fact, we'd always happened? had crammed mass with
something as slight, in-

substantial as itself? toy, then, in
that thicket
of

curls, minutiae of
instances. for pressed the membranes web, bunch
towards their
own
oblation. there, where the wind itself would
swarm, viscous as

honey, you'd let your breath
rush, murmuring, through its very mirrors. yes,
there,
there, once
again: within, that is, the with-

out: chins wedged, knees locked, would wrap massive,
wouldn't you,
a-
bout so
much sudden
pulsating dissemination.

A PENULTIMATE GRAMMAR

that there be a pamphlet, thinner
than
paper, printed in a long-
since ob-

literated typeface. that there be
nothing, finally,
but

tendon, mnemonic tissue, the im-
print of those
ir-

reducible breath-
screens we'd risen to, exulted in,
our bodies lashed to
the

very syntax they'd once, in so
many syncopated measures,
secreted.

BARROCO: AN ESSAY

1

earth but the underside, now, of its
    own scuttled reflection, dwelt, didn't
you, in the neither, the
non-

word, the interstice in which the lips, once,
drew sustenance from the
viscera of
each

radiant
emanation. scrollwork, you'd called it, the
organs wrapt
with-

in that of
their very resonance, the structure conceived
as a single, un-

interrupted sequence of reciprocal
re-

verberations.

                    had weighed shadows, hadn't
you? tested air for its
slightest,
resilient particles. in these parts, the
arms beg

only for echo; the
muscles, the least outlines
of

murmur. roll, though, against
what? read, in the ocherous coils of a
fresco's

flaking
pigments, whose
sustained, perfectly cogent, all-encompassing
sub-

stantiations?

2

you, but
you, but the un-
remitting *replicata* of your own

in-
voluted self. moved, didn't you, through the
blown foam of so much
broken

grammar. there, in
those disseminated spaces, was
'thirst,' you
wondered, still a word? a quantity? for
words, once,
were ladders, scaffolds, the props and stays of
their own

ev-
anescent volumes.

hold, then, to each
abandoned ellipse; crouch within the
wobbling contours of so much
muffled
e-

laboration. for here, at least, once
happened: heard
it-

self happen. yes, here, just
here, for instance, once hung, polyphonous, a
vaulted dome, and, within, a
bevy of bright,
ray-

shaken stars, modulated on
breath a-
lone. feed, then, on
aftermath. yes, sip, residual, from so much

vacua. for the hollow droplet still
re-
tains, as if
resonant, its very emission. listen, then. yes
listen. glean from the

silence, silences. and, so doing,
quench yourself on the
emptiness
of

each parched, irreparable
instant.

•

TRANSPARENT ITINERARIES: 1996

is only the veil that isn't invisible.

only the fluttering scarves of feature, gesture, speech: what go on claiming, nonetheless, their very own autonomy.

no word, therefore, that's not —essentially— misnomer.

no syllable that you wouldn't trace, if you could, to its point of pure emanation.

perceive, that is, in its auroral lustre.

for creation, each time, implies anteriority; implies entry, re-entry into those earliest alphabets, first languages.

reaching —through your own mass— towards their distant lucidities.

always an 'elsewhere' that *isn't*, a 'there' that's *not*, while, out of the very midst of the 'here,' an infallible instinct infallibly points.

held, as we are, to that singular intuition.

"il faut que l'image nous manque."

"that that which allows us to see goes on creating, within each of us, a desire to apprehend that very invisibility." (*Marie-José Mondzain*).

little more, then, than signifiers in search of significance.

of a lost adequation.

(breathing, as we go, whole corridors before us).

. . . laying, within a plethora of
shadows, those
hard sparks: 'phonemes,' you'd called them, what
hissed, needle-
thin, through the very depths of
that dark
air.

---

yes, words in pursuit of words.

through the intermediary of so much murmur, the vectors of our own sumptuous abductions.

instances, that is, of pure transmutation.

(eros but elsewhere).

yes, that very flight which, in narrowing, accelerates towards passage.

towards all that disarticulated letter.

(letter's antecedents).

wherein would vanish and reappear, dissolve and resuscitate within that single, indissociable instant.

return —as if afresh— out of those absconded mirrors.

. . . yes, you
who'd only existed
within so much sonorous reflection, you
who weren't, who would, who'd
sometimes happen
be-

tween resonance and
recoil, breath and
the

simultaneous retraction of its least,
facetted
particle, would sip shadow, wouldn't
you, from long straws
of

sound, suck cloud out of the
cloud's blanched
in-

flections.

---

for the words, the ur-words, outlast —you'd learnt— their successive effacements.

outlast, indeed, the very 'things' themselves.

yes, here, in the late world, in the midst of so much self-generated ephemera, only they, finally, continued to substantiate.

instigate.

allowing the rocks, thereby, to rest within their wobbling vocables.

the wind within the wind's.

while the blown heart —you might have written— went on gathering, in its glass shell, its own scattered whispers.

GARDE FOU

like a figure, wind-
    blown through some Japanese woodblock, its
umbrella
broken, you'd held
to the thin rail of rhetoric, its makeshift

conveyances. *walls, corridors, vistas.* you
who'd hover
in the hollow of
some inalterable resonance, rushed buffeted, now,
through your breath's

deserted stations. has the heart
edges? clouds, a
lost architecture of their own? was there a
'where,' a
'where-house,' a
world that we hadn't yet

in-
vested? had you worked, finally, past your last

definitions? here, you'd say: here, here's a
shed, all
tin, clapboard, asbestos: a
hovel at the outskirts'

outmost extremities. hold it cupped, if you
can, within the
shell, the
wizened crypt of some possible
audition. gland, glow-word, indissoluble property a-
mongst the
pre-

empted, blow it out, now, over your
palms. watch it root, if it
will,
lustrous within the cracked heart of your hands.

ODÈSS

for John Felstiner

long after the evictors had
vanished, you'd gone on fleeing, hadn't
you, avoiding even
your own latticed reflections, as if a
land existed, *una*
terra promesa, past memory itself.

---

the higher the terrain, the
more acerbic the
revelation. here, where berries jingle, brittle
as glass, you're nothing more —you know— than
this palm of whispers, puff of
seed in the sterile fields of the irresonant.

---

coming, as you had, long after the
disasters, you'd cherished residue: cinders
and dust, the still-
disintegrating particles of the verb-
reverberant, breath the rose, once,
cratered echoic.

---

to know, finally, you'd
have to go, travel there, take the
full measure of its
nubilous, tin-white expanses, learn
that you're the sum, now, of its every
exacted eradication.

---

already, the shoots of the peach trees, a
virulent pink. who'll recognize the
hum of their own cells, the very immensity
of their empty message, now that the moon's
added itself to this merciless decor?

---

nowhere's too far, you'd
written, if the fingers a-
light amongst letters, and the letters,
bearing the weight of their own impression, still
smoulder with must.

BREATH'S SUCCESSIVE VERTEBRAE

. . . kept, ever since, a
continuous distance,
a
deep remove from your own in-
nate susceptibilities. rooms, doors, windows: yes,
would face, now, what-

ever perspectives might, eventually,
re-
tain, withhold you, those un-
impaired vistas, for instance, onto the thick,
leafy masses of so much
wavering

re-
flection. would enter, wouldn't you; slake on the
heave of all those
wet,

ligated facets. for 'here' is little more, in
fact, than
interim, than that
on-
going hiatus between a past-imperfect and an ever-

suspended
conditional. would sip: yes, extract from
that errant glitter the
linked nodes
of

nexus.   for there's
'*this, this,*' you'd tell yourself: yes, what the
lips would wrest, say, from so many thick,
shimmering beads, the
breath's

suc-
cessive vertebrae.

what otherwise isn't, you'd
written; *who otherwise*

aren't.   no, inhabited nothing, you realized, but a
landscape laid sonorous be-
tween two
in-
determinates.   but a voice, occasionally; but the

shrub of
a

voice; yes, but the very leaves of the
shrub of
that very voice as they thickened —pulsatile— a-
bout a

tongue's
in-
cursions.

THE MEANING OF THINGS

no, wasn't a body you'd
    penetrated but a
rippling sheath of indeterminate features, a
gaze-veil drawn taut,
monodic, there in the very
midst of so

many
otherwise
exhausted, atmospheric particles.

PALMS

. . . under the steady pressure of palms, the
cloud hardens, fills to its
full
hallucinatory mass. there's whispers, if you'd
listen. there's

hearts. who'll read, though, the
immense hoard of so much
vacant
letter, now that the eye's

blinded it-
self
blonde.

OYSTER

. . . was lightning
that set the radium aglow: lime-green on an
otherwise
il-

legible watchface. nothing, you
wrote, that
wasn't paired, coupled: each, each
other's witness, what flickered wet, just
then, over so

many evanescent parts. bunch, but
only for the

oval. rub, rasp; on our own extirpated oils
burn, but only for
the

glint, spark
that
goes on sputtering within the cage of the teeth.

ABDUCTION

. . . no, wasn't us, finally,
who'd transited but our own extrapolated
images: limb of
our

limbs, heart of our
hearts, yes, those frail
hallucinatory fibers we'd blown, their tips
still
writhing through the eye of the

otherwise
un-
viable. 'here,' you'd
implore, 'taste this, touch that.' but no,
wasn't you, any longer, wasn't

us. lay, already, in the sumptuous folds of
that rippling
chimera, eating the
meats, fruits of each other's

echoes. there, where we'd plunge,
plunged only to vanish. wet,
wavering, in those in-

candescent mirrors, what, in fact, burnt
faster than our
breaths meshed, welded to so much wild,
be-

wildering
vapor.

CALLED IT SPACE

. . . like the opening and
closing of
clouds, those volutes, those
vaporous immensities: what, wedged within our own
swollen

reflections, we'd pried, teased, then, finally,
released into so
many all-
en-
veloping masses. roll, that it
billow; pierce, that it

burst, for this, this only is
depth, dimension, the
sheer

susceptibility of each elastic, still expanding
emanation. no, it wasn't
walls, rooms, cities we'd inhabited but,
turgid, the air, that
very

instant, we'd tooled through our very teeth, the
nimbi pumped, pulsatile, out of
each

lacquered muscle. we who'd spoken, once, of
solids, who'd invested in
structure, only thrived, finally, at the
very heart
of

these hollow
expanses. slick
in the midst of so much

luminous vacuity, had knotted convulsive, hadn't
we; hoarded, against our
gathering
contractions, those heavens, those
high, heightened, meticulously scrolled

decors. rise then, and
plummet. for we'd only happen, here, in our own
self-
induced elaborations. only
exult, finally, all

foam and crystals, in this, the
liminal
landscapes of the all-surrounding *isn't.*

In the Name of the Neither

But we have it in such a way as to speak about it, but not say it itself.
And we say what it is not; what it is, we do not say.

Plotinus

Only in directing language relentlessly towards the innermost core of its own innermost silence can we hope to attain a veritable effect.

Walter Benjamin

LA CHARLESSE

. . . once again, the
wheat's
begun floating.   far out, those
shimmering fields, in their annual
re-

suscitations, rise liquescent, irreal.   remind you, don't
they, of all the
many
miracles that had gone, once, to
substantiate sound.   tell, tell yourself, then, to
rocks, ochre, to anything, that
is, that

isn't.   fill, fill yourself on
murmur alone. for out of shadows hadn't shadows first

emerged?   out of the breath's
be-
wilderment, the least whispers quickened? for here,
here, in fact, is never more than
whatever air you'd eaten, that
abstract in

which, metric, you'd
intermittently,
occur.

LUBERON

only there, in the hills'
deepest creases, would you grow, at
last, legible, hear
your-

self happen in each dark
spark-
hearted foliation.   weren't you, after
all, your very
own antecedent, the organs you'd

bring, mumbling, into that
arena of
leaves, thistles, ledges?   there, that
is, where your breath, at
last, might
en-

counter mass?   wed, then, the interval of
each
articulated
instant, the acorn that

glows, as if epiphanous, at its own
ac-
cording.   for only the pleat,
finally, speaks.   and, in the name of the
neither, resonant,
echoes.

OF OUR INVISIBLE ANATOMY

. . . no, it's not history that
happens, but the
blown veils of so much random apparition: but the
glints, you

called them: the sudden
sporadic drops of some otherwise
in-

determinable substance.   yes, signs, *sema*, all the
given indices of that
all-
pervasive *isn't*.   does it glow?   then
gather.   flutter?   then bring yourself flush a-

gainst the
rippling sheath of such steady dis-

semination.   (whose eyes, you wrote, weren't
eyes but
echoes.   whose echoes but the residue of some long-

since rescinded determinant).   sleep, then, in
mouths, in the open
o-

rifice of so
much
scuttled letter.   feed, feed on
omission alone.   for there, at least —limbs
piled, breath

locked— you'd
glut, occasionally, upon the
verb's
stray vapor, rippling —steadily— along cognition's very edges.

ON IMMINENCE: AN ESSAY

is only what's ahead of us that holds us to the 'here.'

only the isn't-yet that irretractably is.

—star wobbling against the forehead of the eventual—

(our naught-magnetic).

towards which the worked muscles —reciprocal— would thicken.

by the bias of arms, shoulders, teeth, still grappling, penetrate.

(the *isn't*, that is, in all its seething effervescence).

where otherwise were little more than the blown phonemes we'd interpolated from all that ambient impalpable.

but the violence of so much semantic retraction.

that scattered set of cognitive facets we'd come to call world.

each pronoun therein cast to another's exclusion.

the present but the product thereof.

while, uninterrupted, the horizon-line went on writhing. went on tugging at the senses well past the parameters of sense.

---

wherein our hearts
    had first fastened themselves to
glints, sequins, to so many
dark
sparkling insinuations, growing as we had, not
with knowledge, but
thick bubbles of
thirst.

---

where bodies, once, enveloped in cloud, had gone on longing for one another even in the midst of their successive gratifications.

'here' but the postulate for that incipient 'then.'

wherein all altars, all offerings, had been laid in favor of the forthcoming.

wherein nothing, really, but the 'would.'

the memory —fading in the very instant it forms— of that singular anticipation.

. . . kneeling as we had, finally, to
no one, feeding abundantly off so much
in-

consummate, while drawing —like
fortunes— our

sparse reflections from the
broken foam of
such an
all-
but-forgotten constant.

ROMANESQUE

. . . only through the narrows, those adored
particulars, had you ever entered
im-

mensity: moved, even for an
instant, through all
that

disseminated volume. ‘architecture,’ they’d
once called it, those sudden
a-
lignments, that stress, that pressure, the
breath brought tangent to its
very

depletion. wasn’t ‘neither’ what they’d
meant: there, that is, where the
vaulting touched, but only
for its

keyed
re-
leases.

TOWARDS A GRAMMAR OF EXCEPTIONS

. . . in the very midst of history, you'd attempted to
write yourself out, tracing as you
went a
grammar of exceptions, running in
verba transgressiva through the otherwise long-

since al-
lotted.   as if, you'd written, a
whole world lay wedged, vibrant, within some minuscule
linguistic
over-

sight.   between, say, one tense and another: one
articulated breath-
particle and
the
next, the heart —at last— might have its garden;
intent, its

intention.   mull, then, amongst the intervals, those
mute units
of
cognition.   between, say, a
given *this* and a postulated *that*, test
tension, resistance, volatility.   prize, from such

silences, the first
shivering syllables of the yet-
un-
qualified.   for hadn't time itself
once warped to

those releases: the very stars
burst
radial out of so
much measured attribution? for within, you'd
written, would lie the
with-

out. pencil scribbling at the
earth's very edges, yes, a stub amongst the utterly
ex-
tenuated, would tease, if
you could, your breath past, positing this, this

empty dictum in the very
midst of some
yet
emptier expanse.

FRESQUE

. . . nothing
was what their muscles ground at, what they
straddled —momentous— all
buttocks and

breasts within the fastness of that dilapidated
plaster. wouldn't the scrolled clouds, the
puffed shrubs themselves
draw from that
un-

suckled drop? teeth, too, and the
utter silence of
all
that exhortation: yes, theirs,
theirs, once again, asking so much more out of
something that,

nebulous, is
never more than that much unremitting naught.

LIBRETTO

hardens to the spill of
so much soft
ambivalent breath.   fits twisted about each successive
ex-

halation.   aren't we, in fact, for working our-
selves out-
ward,
sipping one another into the utterly un-

differentiated?   knot and
tug, pull and
slip, aren't these the tiny, augmentative gestures we'd
drawn
from that illegible libretto?   for here, where the

room, the
very walls have lost all
substantiality, the mirrors in
swelling blossom.   blossom vacuous.   yes, here, as our
mouths

break open, and our lashes
clamp shut against that very acceleration, we, at
last, massed, culminant, might arch and, in
arching, un-
happen.

TRANSPARENT ITINERARIES: 1997

where the numbers, finally, ended in nimbi.

where rubbed, palpated, the face, finally —cupped in a fanned chalice of fingers— glowed as if exempt, now, from every given contingency.

like a goldbeater's sheath —you'd written— meticulously tooled.

like a mirror, too, but a mirror that had sucked, drained from that very face its every circumstantial feature.

wherein the room itself, that instant, might have volatilized.

---

we, who'd always compared things to the
    comparable, when elsewhere, when otherwise, when
nothing, really, but the
dissolving that
drew.

---

but the relapsing facets of nomenclature.

the decor having grown, if anything, more and more elaborate to the extent that it withheld —within its running pleats— the pleatless.

(its compressed releases).

to the extent that a single earring —its nacreous globe— might have turned premonitory.

a wrist in a bracelet of shadows, inductive.

for only there, exchanging weights, slipping through the very last layers of identity, had we ever happened.

---

hard
hallucinatory splendor of
    those instances: hollow, immense as the
very air in which, still
spasmodic, they'd readily dis-
sipate.

---

within, that is, the *isn't* without which *—de facto— aren't.*

without which, matte, irreflexive, caught in the drafts of a massive reflu-ence, had done little more than thrash within the dry pools of reason.

beating, as we did, against our very depthlessness.

—depth itself but the pure product of a psychic imperative, having no other validity than the satisfaction of that imperative—

by which, counter-syntactical, we'd always acceded.

. . . word
sloughing word in an ever-
al-
leviative movement towards . . .

for only the inference, finally, mesmerized.

only its articulated omission —its blanched letters— drew.

(the sheer beauty of such bewilderment).

limb lapping limbs but only for the sake of that singular passage.

that blind perspective.

wherein, thoroughly enveloped, would reflect —finally— each other's in-
visibility.

STAIRWELLS: THE DISSOLVING STEPS

. . . muscled about our own hoarded diffusions, taut
to so much abundant
un-
telling, told one another 'tooth' and
'shoulders,' yes, 'all the

honey that undulated, that very instant, over the
torso, thus glutted.' now, then,
and

naught. here, then, and —radiant— our each con-
summated
negation. we who'd
crouched, fondled, fed on such wild
elixirs, had tunnelled air, hadn't we? rammed light with
something

al-
together lighter yet. yes, drafts, flues, all the
spiralling conduits of the
sublime-
illegible. weren't these, indeed, the
very

stairwells of some
ob-
fuscated way? what gaunt, condemned, the *illuminati*
once took to? *(little more, now, than*
wind, shadow, updraft. than the
wind's

stacked cirrus in which the
knuckles themselves
would have come
un-

numbered).

here, then, but the base of that
sumptuous
un-

viable. but the
bunching of letters against their own ineluctable dis-
pelling. all history, herein, but abey-
ance; all
holdings, agreements, the heart's
sworn oaths but the swollen globe of so much

dis-
tended tissue. wherein, nonetheless, would
utter. would number each

dis-
mantled step, postulating as we went on the riser and
tread, the sheer thrust of such an

obliterated structure. oh sputter of syllables in the
aftermath of

all sound, amber in which the
air itself, for even an
instant, might
idle.

IN WAY OF INTRODUCTION

poems are about.   yours, though, it
would seem, are
a-
bout the process of their own
depletion: about, one might assume, the sheer a-

boutlessness of being.   oh nexus of
nobody's, *nulla* in the knotted
musculature of
its

very mirrors: is what, vaporous, the lids would
with-
hold; seal, if only they
could, beneath the coil of their

pressed lashes.   tell, tell the tongue, then, to
its shadows; the
long-

boned breath to its troughed
chaotic landscape
of
linen.   for here, here's what we'd wrought to its

very
effacement. oh blown
effigy, what matters, finally, isn't to be written.

NULL'S LAIR

. . . for all that rippling emanation, were the
pleats, the
in-
voluted nodes you'd entered, the deployed particulars a-
dored. who'd spoken of light
meant, in

fact, light's retention; the clouds, voluminous, tucked
underneath the tongue's
tongue-

chosen vocable; of the thighs wild, rioting, their deep
secreted
crypt. the null's lair, you'd
called it: the
nullus itself wrapped, as if reliquated, with-
in its

taut contractive tissues. pry, tease, elicit. there,
though, whatever quickens would only
vanish; whatever hardens
only dis-

sipate in the slap and heave, in the vacuous attempt to
ex-
tract out of nothing
some
substantiating 'something.' yes, you, who'd

pull flowers, fleece, the
breath's
braided shadows free from that
ob-

durate knot, linger, now, in the
loop and
flow, in the in-
audible meander of the air's
vacant octaves: the drift, that is, of that single, ir-
repressible instant; what knows, indeed,
neither

antecedent nor
sequel.

MADRIGAL

only in that gaze's
      long, grey, oscillating corridor had you ever
chased your-
self
down, come impacted a-

gainst so many abrupt
weight-
less particles. foam, fracture: for even the
shadows languish, it would seem, after
so

very little, crouching as they do before the fresh
dis-
positions. were othered to what, whom, you
wondered, if not that
ubiq-

uitous *isn't.* yes, you, who'd
gone on sipping, nonetheless, at lobes, the swollen
folds, as if you hadn't under-
gone, only

moments earlier, that
in-
eluctable preemption yourself.

BLUE MOON

for Peter Cole

“there’s a blue moon in
    blossom,” he writes you from Yerushalayim.   “its
scent,” he
tells you, “rises clear into the crisp, mid-

Hanukkah cold.”   doesn’t the poem, that
address without *destinataire*, do exactly the
same: rise, that
is —sputtering flare— fueled by nothing other than

its own open
im-
perative?   what’s emptier, though, than
words?   than the clattering syllables of so much
precluded existence?   only the
scent, you

realize, yes, the indelible
odors of that
il-

legible scent.   isn’t it for this, this
octave-
without, that one
writes?   why, this morning, amongst its
floating bars —yes, its impossible promises— you reply.

FROM A MIMOSA SKETCHBOOK

. . . of flowers, the year's
very first, these vaporous clusters, fresh
from the coast, weigh little more than your own
floating syllables, their
am-
bulatory chords.

---

filled your sketchbook, all
January, with mimosa, those fat
frothy bunches of minuscule
gold flowerheads.   does anything matter, finally, but
loss, losing yourself to the redolence of those ev-
anescent oils.

---

more like foam, their tiny
globular buds; like feathers, their long bi-
pinnate foliage (where you, who'd sought nothing more
than inclusion, scanned the
density of so much metaphor in search of
some narrow, all-but-obstructed passage).

. . . icy that
scent, almost acidulous that
hoard
of blown gold.

---

more like berries than
blossoms, these fire-beads —a cold
citrine yellow— float
on long pallets of wind.   who, whose, though, unto
what altars, so much effusion laid if
not no one's at the very heart of no one's
obliterated name.

. . . fluffy, their
glowing buds turn brittle, ocherous, but
only for the
pollen's sake (that puff of

ephemeral
whisper that
goes —in turn— to perpetuate the verb).

---

the beauty of mimosa, of
all flowers, finally, resides in the
commotion they provoke, that barbed, be-
wildering disorder that sends you, each
time, to the far, the facing side for the
spectacle of some all-
too-fleeting placation.

RELIQUIAE

that even the earth's least increment, properly housed, might express the transmissive.

charred particles, their vacant flame.

enshrined, for instance, in narrow lanterns of interlocking facets, might speak —occasionally— in place of the speechless.

only though through the conduit of so much bone, shred, unauthenticated splinter.

so much detritus, that is, luminously invested.

wedged pneumatic.

the *nearly-not*, that is, in its immediate —its massive— affiliation with the *nihil*: the all-consummate *not* itself.

(the very vector thereof).

. . . was why the
breath eddied, pooled
a-
bout so little, lingered in the

black
elastic lacquers
of the shadow.   no, not for that
stray in-

candescent gaze, but that the
breach, the

cleavage therein, be glutted; the
interval, for all its

fugacity, at
last, impac-
ted.

TRANSPARENT ITINERARIES: 1998

for Michael O'Brien

. . . here, once again, at
year's end, you rendezvous with
fracture, severance, with those signs that, vehement,
lead —ineluctably— onto
the

flaccid landscapes of their own
dis-
solution.

---

the very spaces we'd peopled, once, with seraphs and dragons, with fork-tailed water nymphs, in default of which a silent hysteria had all too insidiously arisen.

eliminating, as it did, the very mechanisms of attribution.

(inference, now, confined to the inferrer; desire to each of its disassociated parts).

wherein, once, had fabricated wings.

elaborating, as we had, a space every bit as imperative as it was, by nature, illusory.

for 'here,' heavy with foliage, with the wild dicing of our own exhausted syllables, was never more than what the breath —the breeze, that is, within the iris of the breath— had transfigured into the first tenuous outlines of an irrecusable 'there.'

—of those hallucinatory residues: the hard mirage—

wherein were. wherein was.

wrapped, that is, all muscle and murmur, about the rippling screens of the *wasn't.*

unto the nothing —sumptuous— foresworn.

enveloped, enshrined, but only for the length of our own tenuous spellings.

. . . otherwise but a
squabble of blue jays in the black
wind-
struck orchards, but the

shatter, the
spillage, the unremitting dismemberment of each
diaphanous
facet.

---

was only in the ruins, occasionally, that you'd awakened.

only there, in enumerating artifact, cataloging all that auroral debris, that you'd intuited —your ankles jingling with shadow— the first stuttered increments of passage.

wresting out of the forgotten the yet inexpressible.

real as leaves and every bit as evanescent as whispers, what —at last— might track intention: everything, that is, that's ultimately *meant.*

---

darker towards dawn, the
page, that
very moment, is nothing less than the face's
first

hesitant apparition, its
vaporous mask, gradually, filling with

feature.   for whatever speaks, finally, trans-
figures.   fortuitously struck, the
note opens on
the

deep scroll of a mouth, and the mouth, upon the
roundness of its own
in-

cipient response.

APPROACHING THE MILLENNIUM: A LITTLE BOUQUET

for Tedi

. . . .

. . . wherein the roses, this
morning, muscled in the folds of
their own re-

lapsing facets —but the
resonant shells of
some long
a-

bolished signal— break, at
last, out of utter
exhaustion, into
blossom.

LANGUEDOC

. . . rolling in gold
isometric sections, autumn's troughed vineyards
foam to the
oaks'

very edges.   you who'd
squeeze fire, plumb shadow —no, not for their
words, but for the words' all-
but-

obliterated antecedent— enter, now, into light's
last
lingering retreats.   weren't
'moss,' 'mistletoe,' but notes, once, struck
off that utterly

elusive instrument?   viol that set air itself to
so
many vibrant particles?   runs, runs now to
the very fingertips,
that

twinge, that thin
il-
legible tremor: the sputtering residue, perhaps, of
a vocable empty, receptive e-

nough, once, to
be-
get.   you who'd listen, who'd hear, who'd
linger in the wash of

this spent episode, while cherishing, as you
did, something
al-
together lesser yet.

THE HEART, TOO, GOES UNTITLED

the richer the veils, the deeper, more absolute, the penetration.

as if it were that, only that —those sumptuous decors— that conferred depth, dimension and, *de facto*, the materials thereof for their very violation.

just there, that is, where the least glance might have turned to corridor, and corridor —impetuous— to admission.

—chambered, the self's chambered—

about which, flaccid, irresolute, the very air (called it 'the world itself') as if lay in the scaffolds of its shimmering chimera.

there, that is, wherein you'd quicken.

would narrow but only towards each discrete succumbing.

in the verbless depths, that is, of the verb's relinquishment.

for wasn't it language —the very depository of that very decor— that had led you infallibly *towards*; the phrase, perfectly articulated, that had brought you, each time, *unto*?

flush, that is, against that impacted silence; there, where signifier might, at last, coincide with signified.

and signified, with its own inherent incommensurability.

all, indeed, about our own undoing.

about the limbs glistening as they entered, now —so much massed statuary— the labor of their own unlettering.

(wedging, as they did, syncretic).

only there, though. only in the wobbling reflections of that all-obliterating mirror, muscled.

within the nimbus, that is, of a limitless vacuity, ensconced.

where world, in the depletion of its alphabets, out of the disparate splendor of its myriad parts, might cone convergent.

wrap vaporous.

and breath, at last, find itself enveloped within the folds of so much rippling luminescent tissue.

---

weren't the bracelets that
be-
guiled, but the promise thereof, but the disks half-
twisted in

that languorous state of semi-
suspended
an-

ticipation; but the gaze, just then, as it lingered, as
if floated buoyant on the bars of
some prolonged
e-

quivocation.   how we
toy with

immensities, tease history to the very tip of a single
lacquered
strand.   we're only here, though, for
our own
en-

gulfing. we,
who'd rasp shadow, drain whisper, who'd chase the
heart, that riot
of

pulsed muscle, down to a deep
epi-
phanous nothing.

A BLUE-OBLITERATIVE

balustrades, and —just beyond— a blue-
obliterative, taut to the haul of its
chopped currents.   'screen,'
they'd

called it, those
scriptless wastes, there
where the parched lips, irremediable, had
gone un-

lettered.   whose token glows, you'd
ask?   what word with-
stands the

sheer acuity of such
an assimilation?   you, your knuckles coiled
a-

bout some illusory guardrail, utter the
silence that, alone,
still

echoes.

A SELF-PORTRAIT IN LATE AUTUMN

. . . through that ever-
expanding interval, were never more
than these
late bees you'd
scribble: what hung, like sucklings, from the

fat
dangling clusters; than these desolate verb-
studded landscapes you'd
murmur, even
hiss into

some other, some ever else-
where's
ear.

ON AN INSTRUMENT WITHOUT NAME

nature being number, and
   number, in its ebullient disorder, the very spores of
sound, had sought, therein, the
lost radicals of some
late

ideation.   holds but
hardly, you write.   holds, but only by the slenderest
caulicles of a once-
in-

dissociable determinant; by its
least
released seedlings.   drift, then, through
those teased frequencies.   there, where even flight's
in

flight, feed upon the fugue's each
decimated
measure.   for blown, the
particles catch, flare.   all's there; all's

well, you write.   all's, at last,
restored, if only the
heart

enter the
fingertips, and the fingertips,
faultlessly, strike upon their each obliterated chord.

AUTUMNAL

. . . there where the last
rattling
vine-
leaves had let go, you'd sought, in the
ensuing vacuity, the

errant particles of some lost
re-

joinder: its dark sparks cradled in the
very drift of
its
syllables.   write, but only to

read.   read, but only to interpolate the
light's
il-

legibility.   you,
who'd
combed shadow, knelt, now, before the very

interstice.   riddled clause, raucous
ash, only the absconded, finally,
sub-

stantiates.

A PORTRAIT OF

. . . as flesh, suddenly, catches in the teeth of
image, you feel yourself fill to its
least
released pleat, the
undulant folds of its gradually
un-

ravelled fabric.   writhe, then, through all
that illusory muscle, toy in each of its
still
resilient creases.   for there, at last, you'd

enter absence, wrap massive about the
densities of
that very instant that
isn't.   yes, arms, the exact replica of

arms; hair, the hair's great
un-
shaken aureole: there, just there, in that
foaming ap-

parition, you'd fuse, finally, with something far
lighter than
any-
thing the
breath might spell or the limbs, meticulous, measure.

APHONICS

as if, together, we were little more than the base materials —the flushed pigments— for a portrait that —prodded, cajoled, teased irrepressibly forth— vanished in the very instant of its realization.

leaving us, as it did, in the wake of our own effluence.

'aphonics,' you'd called it.

the stripped petals, husked shells of a grammar that, in growing inaudible, only increased in radiance.

words-without-words, the very dimensions thereof.

was there, you wondered, a substance more cherished? in its very inaccessibility, more coveted?

wherein each cognitive cluster found itself ground, pulverized; in the very process of its own impacting, massively dispersed.

only, though, for the sake of the fresh distributions.

for, that is, the breath-to-be.

while basking, as we did, in the shower of all that effervescence; in the manna of its each, discrete, seminal particle.

and felt, therein, our limbs —in relapsing— as if lacquered in naught.

TRANSPARENT ITINERARIES: 1999

that interval, you wrote, between the inadequacies of the given and the imperatives of the inferred.

(that additive without which isn't).

---

through that veil, that
billowing gauze, that interface with face-
lessness it-
self.

---

language: a density, you'd called it, in the service of its own evanescent releases.

fabricating as it went the otherwise inaccessible.

---

was always in the
    elsewhere, wasn't it: in the
rented rooms of those
out-

lying districts that you'd begun drafting the
portrait; begun restituting —feature by feature— its
oblit-

erated mirrors.

---

as if destiny weren't the unraveling of some predetermined dictate but the patient reconstitution of the intended.

the resuscitation of so many suppressed ur-words by the bias of a yet-to-be articulated grammar.

(what lay secreted within the parched hollow of our each and every exhalation).

was why you'd lowered yourself into those ruins, wasn't it? why you'd tape-measured whatever vestiges remained in an attempt to interpolate — from their least sequential sections— the full thrust of such an obfuscated dynamic.

. . . were roots, the white irises', you'd
discovered, that had
blinded the
idol's
eyes.

---

far too late for anything, now, but those earliest ideations.

the unearthing, therein, of the eventual.

wasn't this why the bodies grappled the way they did? cherished the incipient against their own ineluctable depletions?

their teeth bared; their breath broken.

why, too, you'd have uttered —just then— that word without words: that elision glittering in the very midst of so much spent syntax.

and heard, so doing, the silence —thus solicited— sound.

VACANT ARCHITECTURES

for Andrew Joron

dissolved walls of the reverberatory.

against which, once, the sensate particles sparkled. . .

being, indeed, our vis-à-vis with nothing if not, under certain privileged circumstances, the rippling partitions of so much hallucinatory volume.

the vacant architectures, that is, in which, momentarily, had felt ourselves substantiated.

. . . as if, finally, vouchsafed. . .

what, in fact, the murmur alone would have emitted: cast prismatic across the contours of the otherwise inexistent.

rendering, thereby, the *nullus* incarnate.

. . . there where the roses of happenstance, on their
blown octaves, opened out onto their own
rose-
less expanses, a
volute, as if *de facto*, came to cup, therein, their very
ef-
fulgence.

—incommensurable halo of a cellular determinant—

in default of which had begun grinding our syllables to an irresonant dust,
nourishing ourselves upon exactly those substances that had allowed, once,
the naught to flourish.

and the breath, therein, to fresco its very phantasmagoria.

. . . was what, in the throe of its particles, had
stunned the
in-

determinate with
scintillae: there, that is, where the syllables, at
last, had settled that the
un-

bidden, in
ex-
foliation, might glow.

ARTICLE OF FAITH

. . . would travel forever
towards those buried mirrors, what the future
so
consummately withholds. 'memories,' you'd
called them: the

grey gaze in its diadem of
dark lashes
a-

lighting, at last, in the remote ovals of the
eventual. does it glow? then
glean. ripple? then
ride the

least quivering signal clear to its
deepest
ob-
fuscated source. for only the
image —'icon,' you'd called it— withstands the
un-

remitting dispersion of the
heart's
most adamant particles. move, then, amongst
shadows. in the
pale grammar of the grasses, read the
re-

constituted facets of the otherwise
ob-
literated face. nothing
ends.

The Places as Preludes

There's a note of a certain nameless black in the restless gusty blue of the broad sky, and, in vibrant contrast, the poppies' bright vermilion. —Vincent van Gogh *for Beatrice & Beatrice*

PRELUDE I

would begin anywhere, wouldn't you, as
if there
were still there, and you
still yourself in this phenomenological drift to-

wards some all-but-
il-

lusory absolution. *scintillae,* you'd
called them: those
sudden stations: shrines that the gaze makes in
eddying
a-

bout a palmful of pebbles. do the distances
ever end? does the
air, at
last, resonate at its own
according? work, then, those
scuttled expanses. there, where thirst alone

constitutes measure, would memorize, as you
went, what, in

so many sequential sections, you'd never
yet
heard.

PRELUDE II

. . . the late rays, already, eclipsed in
leaves, you'd
ex-
change places with yourself: assume, if only
you could, the

open vocable. round, though, to
what, you'd
ask yourself, for the tongue's

lapping at shadow, nourishing itself on
after-

math alone. didn't the bones, once, in their
jeweled boxes, as if
blossom? pollinate, so doing, the

very air itself? room after room, you
move, now, through
replica: the irrecusable dictates of the
self-
reflexive. is it the lymph, then,

that tugs? that, pulsatile, emits the
il-
legible message? that keeps the moon

coursing through its ideogram, and the ideogram,
pallid, in-
distinct, beyond all
cognition?

PRELUDE III

had never met, had you? never
would, either, you
well realized, even if sometimes you'd as if

grazed, one
against another, in the magnetic affinity of
mass for its
in-

audible murmur. no, not
even there, amongst the bright tables and taut
wind-
struck linen, had you once detected the least

evanescent signal. why, then, this
insistence? why should the bodies grapple, pile,
beat as they do
a-

gainst such
manifest omission?   what, in fact, does the
breath, in its running braille, interpolate that the
lips, in

paraphrase, never
could?

TRANSPARENT ITINERARIES: 2000

all but prelude to the inaudible.

all but flues, updrafts. grammar itself, in its inherent dynamic, aspiratory.

as, one after another, the words come to defer.

. . . there's nothing within that
doesn't predicate the
with-
out; no limb, no foliated muscle that

doesn't wrap adamant a-
bout its own
ab-

solving. issues but
only in the
un-

utterable simplicity of its wrought
releases. there, that is,

where the breath, at last, comes to
kneel, and
the
fumes —in sputtering— to ascend.

---

altar, *altaria,* the tabular base plates of the ascensional.

populating air as we have with impalpable anatomies.

such as that of bodies that can't be touched: only projected, diffused.

paradis peint, où sont harpes et lus.

'causal' you called those heavens as, so doing, you huddled within a universe of devolving effects.

subject, as such, to a virulent literality.

(what's gone to desiccate —granulate— the very pigments of that once hallucinatory spectacle).

---

otherwise, only the hard cloud of the
moon, on
certain days, withstands the given
de-

scriptive.

---

only her eyes —far too lustrous to alight, fix themselves upon any predetermined object— serve to introduce those all but absconded expanses.

'reflecting,' as Plotinus had put it, 'backwards.'

there where mass might revert to measure.

and measure, to the incommensurable bars of an incipient harmonics.

. . . where, by working the landscape back-
wards, by
beating volume, contour, to
an essential set of pulsatile rhythms, would re-

suscitate, so
doing, no,

not the verb, but —prefigurative— the
open vocable, locked obdurate, as
it is, within an
orifice of
lips.

QUINCES

1

. . . just as the poem
runs rippling through the poem and
coincides, so

doing, with its
inherent momentum, so the
quince, catching on
its

pinched syllable, rounds to its
mass, decks itself in
a

burst girdle of
gold
foliage.

2

nothing, you'd
noted, that
doesn't happen twice, but only at the

bow's
according.

3

beating, as they do, abrasive, one
against another in an
un-
remitting mistral, these
plump, pendulous mamillaires know
no

quarter if not the
notes themselves, their
deep

refluent receptacles.

4

where else, though, would the
quinces go, would you
your-

self, if not into
those

vibratory under-
worlds: there where the breath, at last,

might find
umbrage.

5

. . . offered unto no
known
deity, these battered
rococo vessels, come September, swell
putrescent. find, then, the
key, the

chord mute enough to record such
numina before
the

ground thuds redundant under so much
broken
token.

TESTAMENT

. . . that part that
goes nowhere, fits nothing, that
doesn't, wouldn't, isn't, instigates none-
the-

less the speculation of all parts that
are. call it, if

one will, a part so
im-
partial, an anomaly so absolute, that
nothing, if not the breath it-
self, might attain

such resolute autonomy. nothing, that is, if
not the

germinal circulation of
letters
a-
lighting, at last, on
something altogether lighter than the

slightest
increments of
substance itself. there, that
is, where the

rose, so
accorded, might bud ebullient in the very
midst of such
an

inherent socket of omissions.

PRELUDE IV

. . . went on resonating, the
myriad fragments of
that dec-
imated mirror. wasn't it that that you heard, now,
rather than

saw? yes, heard: heard the
gaze and the gracious vault of the brows as, ob-

edient to
number, the limbs, as
if accorded, entered, now, the full scales of that

singular fugue. age of
abandon, of
dissolving effects, was only the sonorous, finally,
that with-

stood that
on-
slaught of obliteratives. yes, there, in that

room without walls, would bring, no, not the
lips, but the pressure of their
plump im-

print, setting, as you did, tremor to
treble, there in the
air, the dark air, the air reverberant of this, your
ul-
timate refuge.

PRELUDE V

. . . just as the fugue thinned, finally, to the
blown
gold of its
antecedents, you'd assume —once again— your own

empty
plentitude. yearned, in fact, for
nothing less. for whoever holds the flower
holds, so

doing, the
luminous thread. only, though, in its
un-
gathering could you hope to accede. only in the
filament sipped, get to
glimpse the

tenuous epiphanies. for there, just then, the very
room would vanish: there, that
is, where the
blouse

slid open, offering, as it did, like an opiate, those
plump
obliteratives. what speaks, then, in the
midst of

such sudden effacement? what underwrites the
words, finally, if not the
particles, and
the

particles, that pale incessant manna of
in-
commensurables.

PRELUDE VI

. . . even the wasps, spastic over
still water, partake in
that hallucinatory spectacle you'd gauge, if you
could, set to the
scales of some
ob-

fuscated order. for certainly number
under-

lies the very air itself, throbs obdurate through the
fat
summer squashes. not a note, though, that doesn't
dis-

solve at the least
specious
reading. that doesn't refute, so doing, mis-

nomer. move, then, along the scored corridors, the
thin
quivering
passage your breath makes as it oscillates

with mineral. just there, for instance, where the
cliff
turns liquescent: enters, that is, its
spectrum of

sound, let your tongue lap, slide, punctuate each
given
instance. for earth, earth's

grammatology, remains to be
written.

IN PRAISE OF THE IMPLICIT: AN ESSAY

"To say the unsayable, to open language to its own otherness, shows what is missing in reality." —Andrew Joron

1

. . . who'd ring, from the
shattered syllables, the lost *eloquentia* of
sequence: that all-
but-

obliterated dynamic wherein, once,
had un-

raveled. move, so doing, from the eclectic-
isolate to the
in-

dissociable allusion. from, that
is, *explicitus* to
implicitus: exactly what Fulbecke, in his long-
forgotten *Pandectes,* had so
postulated:

Such thinges as are not verballie
forbidden are implicatiuele permitted.

2

. . . whereupon, on
affinity alone, might find oneself meshed, en-
tangled, interwoven with something other
than one's
own

ir-
recusable self. might, by the bias of every
such

semantic redistribution, exchange particles for
predilectives; feel, as one did, the
cells, still

seething, pour into the matrices of pure intent.

3

there, for instance, where, in a
Aen. IV. 148 circlet of gold, Apollo went to bind (*implicat*) his long
flowing tresses (*crinem . . . auro*), so, too, the
breath, in its
meted de-

ployment, would invest air with all
such
transfigurative increases. just then, for
instance, wouldn't you, too, catch
glimpses? find your-

self included: yes, implicated, within the
released fields
of
inference? fumbling among the bells of the

campanula, no longer wrist and thumb, yet
not
quite flower, would trace, wouldn't you, those

effaced
frequencies (*texturae*, you'd
called them) wherein every instance of the dis-
parate, on the
sonorous looms of
syntax, might integrate, once again, the

sustained bars of the in-
ex-
tricable. no, no longer ankle and calf, yet
not

quite meadow, orchard, and rock, would
enter, wouldn't you, on the
wefts of
sequitur, the inherent dimensions of naught.

INCARNATA

. . . beguile, those
densities in the full array of their
a-

dored attributes, but only for the
sake of

that singular passage. for there, in
those
sipped omissions, where
language, like a succulent, had

thinned to a spent wafer, life, at long
last, might happen: lips
wrapped taut
a-

bout an opulent cloud that no
one, any
longer, need utter.

FLORALIA

. . . way that her eyes slide indolent, as if
re-
calcitrant, against her own
inherent nature. enter, as they do, that

desolate zone on the
far side of
a
rich, horticultural arbor that, brimming with
chaffinch, con-

stituted, once, her
torso. write, then, to
remind her. write to re-
call: hyssop and hydrangea, rose and gardenia:
what, in her

innermost being, had functioned, once, instead of
organ. that her lashes might
a-
light, again, upon all that

floralia, and you, therein, in the quick slip of
her dark, dappled sources, be
granted passage.

THE GOLDBEATERS

"... I would rather be Echo, in love with what she hears."

... ours, autumn's
deep
baroque golds: ours, ours alone, their
para-

digmatic decors (as much the
dense
overlapping foliage of
our voices as that of the leaves them-

selves).

~

would tease from her
tongue its
least

glistening particle, set its every
such fleck to the wefts of sequence: those long-
since-
dis

mantled frequencies.

~

'echo,' pluck 'echo,' of all words, from
so
much proffered ore (as if, indeed, only the

reverberative, in
extremis, could as-
sure such passage: oaks, either side, voluminous, a-
bout our each

secreted
whisper).

~

wherein would tell: tell the world, if we
could, to its own
for-

gotten self. for the boughs
beg telling. beg the
least de-
pleted syllables just as we,

begging our own, would beat light. beat
shadow. down through
the
rattling foliage, bring, at last, our own breath-

im-
pacted bodies to a taut
pummelled
sheet.

SEPTEMBER

for Michel Mayan

. . . now that the Swan
has swung southward on her blue
wind-
beaten pedestal, will the syllables, at long

last, harden? the breath, so
doing, catch on its
lost

dictata? the heavens themselves, as a set of
recondite signals, would release the
ruffled, the winged, the
intuitively
dis-

posed. lactiferous, hadn't she, from the deepest
pleats of
her

being, already insinuated, by her
inclination alone, the
Way?

PROVENÇAL NIGHT

for Tim Bahti

. . . all night the wind, incendiary,
lapped at the
stars, set them wobbling within their deep
phos-
phorescent sockets. no, nothing's too far if it

draws, in-
volves you: takes you past this
fist-
ful of viscera into such in-

commensurable displays. who are you, anyway, if
not the night's
mock
musicologist: he
who'd intuit chord, crescendo and resolve out of so

many swirling
pin-
wheels of fire. yes, out of those

cold smouldering cauldrons —fuchsia, turquoise and
bronze— interpolate the bars of
some all-but-

for-
gotten measure. for you're nothing, really, but the
empty receptacle
of everything you're not. gather, then, and,
in

gathering, orchestrate. pluck Persei and
Polaris,
Betelgeuse and
Bellatrix. for there, only there, in

that basketful of
breath, might the notes, still

molten, strike vibrant and
resonate, so doing, against the shallow ribs of your
yet in-
credulous flesh.

PRELUDE VII

there where the mirrors, suddenly, had turned to
wine: the
auspicious yield, that is, of
those trellised vineyards, you'd entered the

realm of
your own conceits. weren't you, after all, the
one you'd

never met? who'd done little, finally, but
anticipate some all-
but-

unlikely encounter? sip, then, on these thin
dis-

tillations. on their turbaned vapors alone,
trans-
literate. who'd
thumbed pebbles, fingered
grass, would ride, now, the draft of

those transparent pages, your breath, as you
did, shattering like the
husks of so much
gutted
shell.

PRELUDE VIII

there's somebody else here, and it's
you if you'd
listen; tune, if only you could, to those tenuous
frequencies. you who aren't, who
would, who, in

languishing in the vibratory fields of the
in-
cipient, had cherished, so doing, the
treble-

headed insects. isn't anatomy but antecedent, the
cells but seeds to
such

premonitory expanses? would thin as you
went, wrap as you did to that
shroud of
blanched shadow. for
only there, there where the full scale's worked to a

tremor, might you kneel, and, in
kneeling, suckle, at
last, the first
resonant drop.

PRELUDE IX

. . . for the images you'd
mis-
taken for flesh had no sooner flourished then, in-

eluctably, they'd
dis-
solved. only, occasionally, a
scuttled pair of earrings still testified for such an
ob-

solescent etiology. remained, finally, but
residue. but the
sheer remoteness of a world in which, relentlessly,
you'd

sought entry. had the cloud, you asked, come to
replace the

grotto? the ideation, the
hard muscles of
re-

joinder? sleep, then, in the cusp of a whisper. for
there, in
so
many scarcely audible particles, you'd

encounter, at long last, the
impacted magma of
origins if
only, indeed, in the evanescent spray of its pen-

ultimate dis-
persions.

TRANSPARENT ITINERARIES: 2001

for the perfumes, you'd come to realize, were far more substantiating, finally, than the flesh.

the figuration, than the lavishly befigured.

much as the notes, in shivering free of their very instrument, assume an autonomy of their own, so, too, the phrase —under certain conditions— touches upon the scales of an otherwise inaccessible register.

only though —as you'd noticed— by the bias of metaphor, aesthetic confabulation, by a rigorous and unremitting respect for *trompe-l'œil.*

wherein, derelict, the outline of angels —however indistinguishable— continued to transit.

the imaginary wed —as such— to the mnemonic.

---

who'd entered the ring of her own
re-
semblances, matching as she had her gaze to
that in

her mirrors, and her mirrors to
those archaic signals that only reached her, now,
in

sporadic
pulsations.

teased as we are by all that sumptuous expanse: what can only be attained, finally, by means of our own unselving.

shedding as we went —like so many breath-petals— each and every individual predeterminant, but only for the sake of that singular depletion.

unto that irresolvable ore, that ante-matter, magnetized.

. . . having rolled over, as you had, no, not onto
mass but mass's
weight-
less imprint. there, that is, in the all-

too-
apparent slap and
heave —your every muscle fast to its
own im-

paction— would flourish, at
last, the
il-

legible signature.

a scribble of roses at the earth's very edge: what, for all their pungency, *passeth all understanding.*

PRO LYRICA

. . . three pebbles
make a path. the least breeze, though, would
tatter the
wafted strands of
this tenuous syntax, dissipate all sense of the com-

mensurate. wedge, then, to
what if not

these very knuckles. for only there, in taut ac-
cretions, might the moon, in all its
octaves, come to
quaver.

QUESTIONS OF GRAMMAR: I

. . . what with the wind
scuttling through the syllables, that interval you'd
relentlessly
sought —idyll of apples and

oleanders— went unuttered. wasn't that, though,
why you
wrote: to reiterate, that is, what you

couldn't: world that
wedges, presses
be-
tween its flexed members, its

irrecusable
isn't.

QUESTIONS OF GRAMMAR: II

. . . sought fields you couldn't fall through; iron
in the very midst
of

echo. was it, you wondered, the
cornflowers, notorious at those altitudes, that
held you, there where
the

page that
never existed went on burning wordlessly off your
own in-
candescent mirrors.

QUESTIONS OF GRAMMAR: III

. . . was why, once, they'd
brought them, those
ear-
shaped oyster shells: scattered them a-

bout their
expiatory altars. 'hear,' the
shells must have sung, 'hear us,' im-

plored. what, by the sheer
urgency of
such

supplications, had kept the
stars wobbling —misericordious— within their
hard
socketed stations.

THE PHYSICS OF VERSE

for Ed Foster

begins, each time, in obliquity.

in an abrupt, as if convulsive, deflection on the part of the stuttering breath.

violating, thereby, those given constants that —birth-to-death— determine the sheer linearity of an otherwise inviolable trajectory.

(an otherwise irrecusable set of preestablished bio-rhythms).

wherein the poem, at last, might emerge, fueled on little more than the pulsatile insistence of a yet-to-be articulated intuition.

meter, therein, in pursuit of matter.

initiating, from the very outset, its deviate course, accelerating out of an inherent lyric elation or, to the contrary, slackening well below those prescribed cadences to meet the requisites of some impending disclosure.

(its liquescent underworlds).

refractory, in both instances, to the dictates of sequence.

for the poem, out of obedience to its innate centripetency, comes to coil and, in coiling, circumscribe the temporal within the oval of its sonorous reflections.

—its respiratory mirrors—

enshrining as it does —well out of harm's reach— its very antecedents against the dissipate forces of causality.

there, that is, within its vertical chambers, where only origin's, finally, premonitory.

—lily all that 'lily' need ever foresee—

wherein time, turned backwards upon itself, might become, in *contrattèmpo,* time absolved.

and the syllables, so salvaged, effloresce.

PRELUDE X

. . . you, who'd
long since lost track of yourself, wrote for the
indices, didn't
you: the wizened benchmarks at the extreme
edge of those
res-

piratory landscapes. no, no dahlias, no
marigolds, any longer, came to
relieve that

miasmatic expanse; no way, the
way's
blanched trajectory. there, only the deflected, it
seemed, drew; only the obliterated,
magnetized. in the wake, then, of such
massive
withdrawal, would sleep, but where? would read, but

what? troughed in shadow, had
resonance left, at
least, the sparkling residue of some dec-
imated letter? winnow, then,
what-

ever little remains. yes, sip the slightest
vestigial syllable. that the future —that's forever
earlier— might wedge vibratory
be-
tween tongue and teeth.

PRELUDE XI

for Clayton Eshleman

. . . even here, where you'd gotten the
rocks, finally, to rhyme,
rhetoric's

still riddled. won't close, include you in the
blown veils of some lost
ideation. *part,*
partial, partialized. would, if you
could, enter the conjugates: there, that is, where

every instance of
inter-
relatedness lodged, once, in-

violable. wasn't that, in fact, why you'd
threaded stars? tried to catch, in the
cicada's

monodic stridulations, the
stray bars of some
arcane an-

nunciate? for only there: there, that is, in the
world that the
world left out, would the

nimbus, at
long last, wrap —adamant— about its ubiquitous *isn't.*

PRELUDE XII

frivolous with immensity, let your
fingertips slip over the
very contours
of
inception, grazing as they did its pleats, ripples, the

slick
contracted expanse of its muscles, laminated
in

dark oils. loom and
dissolve; heave and succumb. for there, furtive, epi-

phenomenal, you'd only transit —vaporous— through all
those flexed
de-
terminants. does the mirror know what the
mirrored doesn't? wouldn't the

resonance enter, root
resplendent, there where the voice,
manifestly,
couldn't? thus drawn, solicited, even the air's
for

inclusion. so, too —you'd noted— each
dis-
tended member, its least
emitted murmur,
but

only wrapped, enclosed in the whirring viscera of its own
un-
wording. for only then, in its very
ex-

tinguishing,
spoke.

TRANSPARENT ITINERARIES 2002/2003

all you'd ever known had been density; all you'd ever sought: passage.

wherein the body, in pursuit of its lost etiology, would be seen as nothing more, finally, than expedient.

than conduit.

than a flexed assemblage in the service of its own transgression.

grappling as it went for glints, intimations, radiant *insignia.*

. . . there, that is, in those
lost landscapes, where
muscle
would serve as little more than sphincter to
image: sheath within which the
be-

loved, perfectly diaphanous,
slumbered.

---

rare mirror that, rather than reflecting, assimilated.

as if absolved.

wasn't that why you'd adopted that obsolescent vocabulary as you had: idiom in which the verb, once, had managed to shimmy free of its each and every substantive.

and rise, so doing, pulsatile . . .

where, at the extreme outskirts of every such utterance, you'd enter, finally, those empty densities.

no, not by anything you'd have said and, in saying, circumscribed, but — in the nimbleness of each given articulation— vacated.

scientia bene modulandi: that science, as Censorinus had called it, of fine tuning.

. . . being locked into
all
that clattering
canebrake, squinted, didn't you, in search of
interstice: *lapsus* in the midst of
textus for winnowing your

words
through.

---

that they might have alighted, thereby, upon that somnolent figure, lapping as they did at each of her cherished features.

having assumed —at that remove— the exact same properties as those they'd evoked.

the blown heart, the blown lily's.

—their blessed conflations—

while pretending, all the while, that you'd returned to the given, the assumed, the linguistically prescribed.

that the breath might have managed to wrest itself free from the magnitude of such an encounter.

. . . its proffered succulents . . .

that 'here' was still here, and world something other than the fast-fading imprint of something it never was.

PRELUDE XIII

. . . had fallen through the
cloud of your
own
postulates; felt, in the absence of all *im-*

maculata, the
underlying ground
give way. wasn't the wrist, once, the air's

implement; what muscled the
irises in
limp overlapping scaffolds of petal? work,
then, the
hollows, you'd

murmur. for there, where there's nothing to
hear, would round to the
ruins, say, of
a

stray substantive. plumb, as you
did, its
slightest tremor for the least, lingering
trace of some
ob-

solescent adage, spent
an-
nunciate. feed, so doing, on
the rinds —the scattered refuse— of quaver.

PRELUDE XIV

. . . despite the
density of such scent and the blown commotion of
so
much curl, what draws —simultaneously—
dis-

sipates, thins epi-
phanous. isn't this, indeed, that
foam you'd spoken of, that evanescence you'd
sip (if

only you could) to something other than that much
disparate
particle.

archives-in-
air, there
where the sacred, once, got stashed, don't
ask for the *isn't.* wrap,
rather, to

mass. for only there: the muscles
im-
pacted, would the
numinous break free, and —discharged— the
radiance therein, in thin
showers, find
it

self refracted.

PRELUDE XV

. . . there's a certain blue, out
there, you
can walk through. boulders, too, shallow as
grammar, that

yield to your least glance, your flimsiest
rumina-
tions. now, not even the

boisterous pink wildflowers draw, dis-
tract, keep you from this
spec-

ulatory peregrination. you, who'd
tested air against the
dia-
pason of each
meted particle, enter now the proffered organs of

absence. bright hair, sleek
shoulders; who's to

say that the
world doesn't end in
some gratuitous gust of wind but in this, its
cherished
omission?

THE OVAL AS THE OBJECT OF ITS OWN IDOLATRY

. . . the oval, as
ovals will, dreams it-
self, running its cheek against the
puffed cloud of some
fortuitous
pillow.

. . . the moon, all
night, little more than its
mirror, its
celestial accessory.

. . . alludes to nothing, this evanescent
idol, if not its
own
ebullience.

. . . as, to the play of its fingertips,
its lips
spread open and, so doing, the
rich
volutes of its dark lashes
clamp rapturously
shut.

as-
similating, as it does, rockrose and
iris,
hyacinth and
mauve, within the
plump folds of its all-
but-in-
audible murmur.

... no, not even the squirt of
mid-
summer's sudden, self-
extinguishing fires doesn't fall sub-
ject to this,
its
sumptuous envelopment.

... as, fully
em-
bedded, the oval absorbs all notion of
in-
terval within the
troughed knots of its
linen.

. . . and writhes, therein, to the
riotous
scent of its own
suc-
cessive releases, reverberant.

MIRABUNDA

. . . drawn by the
sheer
elasticity of that deep amber gaze, grew weight-
less, didn't you, as if
es-

tranged from tables and
chairs, wind and
glassware: from whatever constituted, once, the
world-at-

large. for there, as if
suspended within
that
dark idol of lashes, it no longer mattered, did
it? taut to

such expanses, sipped
light, sucked shadow, glutted on the letters of that
trans-
parent alphabet. yes, there where the

self, finally, had
lost all consistency, the
breath, at
last, could harden about that sustained bevy of rays.

BUNDLE: IN DEFENSE OF METAPHOR

. . . called it 'bundle' because you'd
en-
velop, if you could, those im-
ponderables within the folds of some literary ex-

pedient; wrap mystery, so
doing, within the tufted conceits of

metaphor. for other-
wise, ambling as you did through the wastelands of the
all-
too-assimilated, saw the clouds as if
clot; each thing, be it
surf, spume, or wind-tattered parasol, grow remorselessly

explicit. how, then, account for what you
couldn't? ring, as if you
could, the ir-
resonant? for there, where the heart, once, stopped (her
hair

flooding her shoulders in a flora of black
arabesques) arose, in-
exorable, that

radiance. no, there's no
holding, with-

holding those inherent vectors. no, nothing if not this
bundle that
isn't, laid before an altar that's
not. for there, in the

name of nothing, really, might arise, periphrastic, these
all-
but-in-
audible murmurs.

NAIAD

. . . as your fingers
fork through that ebullient
black
waterfall, your breath

catches fire. would weld stars, roses, wouldn't
you? bring, if only you could, that
torch of whispers to an
in-

candescent focus. no, the world's
never come closer. closer yet,
though, the lobes and
shanks of

that shimmering figure: what, emerging, now, in a
splatter of
pearls, slips through this
mesh of syllables you'd so meticulously deployed.

MEDITERRANEAN

. . . no, not the surf that
bursts tumultuous over the kelp-impacted break-
water but that that, catching on
so

much di-
shevelled linen, troughs and heaves to the
quick
impulsive slip of
our ankles; the thrust —redundant— of our own
exac-

erbated thighs. against what, though, will the
breath crest, and the heart, in
its
compressed vessel,
break? oh world in the

wake of
worlds : is there, indeed, any other? isn't it that
that in propelling us under urges us
toward? for

there, in that
spume of whispers, in that
in-
distinguishable turban of wedged tendons, elsewhere, in
all its
magnitude, comes to
en-
velop us in the radiance of its own empty reaches.

PRELUDE XVI

. . . towards the Assumption, the
nimbi, in
black updrafts, mass fulgurous. wouldn't you, too, on
your own
re-

lentless unlettering, as if gather? on the wefts of
some
un-

utterable postulate, as if
swell? what, though,
a-
bout the bones, you'd
ask? yes, where would the bones go, catching as they

went on those taut, all-
en-

veloping turbans of ascendent current? tongue
lapping at
ash, would posit, wouldn't you, each of those fresh
dis-

positions. past all
grammatical
fatality: there, that is, in the interval created by so
much

spent particle, would recognize, in the volute of
those e-
volving silences, the imprint of an air that no longer
ballasted but, at last,
buoyed.

PRELUDE XVII

. . . loved rivers as much as
smoke, the
sinuous skeins of a world in the midst of its own
un-

raveling. taste this, touch
that. for hadn't you, too, taken measure,
marked distance, seen the shadows lap a-
brasive at the base of so
much

bold relief? effaced, but unto
what? dismantled,
that
canonical vision wherein the gaze, once, found

refuge, but only for the sake, now, of
some sound-
less remission. for hadn't silence
come to muffle sign, to drain the very stars of
their sparkling
signatures?

                                        kneel, then, to

nothing if
not the numinous in its
bound-
less dispersion: what the breath, merely in

uttering, un-
braids.

PRELUDE XVIII

. . . for the taut, overlapping ligature of the
muscles only serves to
en-
velop the smoke, withhold the roll of all that baroque

effluvia. wedge, then, to
those narrow drafts, the slip of every
such disparate
in-

determinate: the 'abolished alphabet,' as you'd
called it, of a
once
pellucid script. that there, where even the vertebrae
get caught in the
coils of

that
vaporous emission, the
implicit might edge, in meted sections, towards

transmission. blow, then, on
those
choked vocables. tease

intention forth. that each thing, once told, might
resonate, finally, with its
lost
luminosity: there, that is, where the
breath, at the very

end of
its
beaten pilgrimage, might, at long last, squirt gold.

New Poems

(2004–2005)

FROM A GRAMMARIAN'S FIELDBOOK

I

. . . looking for the space
space left out, the
in-
finitesimal oversight in the sealed

ensemble, would toy with
irises, wouldn't

you, the least breach in that limp
over-
lapping peristyle of
blown petals. isn't that

what bodies are for; plucked, their
wrought instruments
brought to an
in-

commensurable tremor? was why
you'd
stuttered as you had as if to utter, so
doing, the wind-

scuttled shadows of everything you couldn't.

FROM A GRAMMARIAN'S FIELDBOOK

II

. . . with elsewhere, now, even
further, had worked the
least
grammatical particle to a fine powder, the

'future passive' to a
thin
pitted whisper. "hear me?" you'd
ask, where no one, any longer, possibly could, the

utterance already dis-
sipated in echo, and echo in the

errant wastelands of the air. was there, then, a
word-
without, something your lips
might round to and, precipitous,

envelop? the vocable, say, of
some
hallowed honey that, no, you'd
never name but could, on certain occasions, sip

FROM A GRAMMARIAN'S FIELDBOOK

III

. . . all that fluffy stuff going on in
mid-
air, while you, as
articulated mass, muttered particles for the sake of
some desultory
self-

assessment. weren't these, indeed,
your only vehicle: the sporadic vectors of an all-but-
exhausted methodology? thinner
the

light, less viscous the
honey, here on these late estates where longing alone
constituted measure. would
tunnel shadow, wouldn't you? extract, from those
drafty corridors, the
thin
crystalline splinters of some

ob-
solescent syntax. no, not one, though, that de-
noted but, in sustained anticipation,
pre-

figured. for even the ruins, however decimated,
harbor the
germ of some radiant
elaboration. so, too, you'd add, do the

words.   do those
broken receptacles that a breath, once, blew out of
some lost
im-

perative. wasn't that
what you'd utter? and, in
so
many stuttered sections, glean, at least, the
                    residue of some all-but-obliterated intent.

PSYCHE

. . . who'd swallowed your gaze, the very
glint of
your heart, there
where it refracted, once, within the
wet rippling pleats of that
ir-

reproachable mirror. wanted your
hands back, didn't you, the pressure your

fingers exerted in
molding earth to the
air's
radiant anatomy. twirled spoons, tapped

shadows, attempted to wean from the
rock those lost
sonorities. were little more, now, than the

residue of that chimeric lustre, the
backwash of what, in
default of
its reflections, had long since

dissolved. bone of your bone, breath of your
breath, how will you recognize your-
self now that that
glow's
gone under?

ACCORDING TO THE OCTAVE

. . . the barley, by then, had
smothered the
poppies; risen profuse, pale jade, over so much
choked
vermilion. hadn't the pages, too, gone

under; speckled, that
hermetic script —what promised, once, to

cure the
world— undergone a like

obliteration? little, now, but shadows to
comb. but the fluffy stuff of
ir-
resolute memory to braid. what, though, if some deep-
seated gland
re-
suscitated? some
obnubilated function secreted, once again, its

sonorous particles? red: yes, red, you'd
say, that
raucous vermilion. wasn't that the color wherein the
chorals first
e-
merged? flourished remedial? for the word's, finally,
with-

out. was why
you'd huddled so, wasn't it? had grazed, as you went, the
walls of the cave,
tapping, no,

not the
mineral, but the pale premonitory contours of the cloud.

SIX QUATRAINS FOR A POSTULATE

. . . however much you
might have loved them, the
clouds, finally, will have you, wrap you in the
loose, un-

ruly skeins of
their swaddling. for you're
muscled to nothing, really, if not the
fortuitous chords you'd occasionally strike, the

iris and
oleander of some long-
forgotten harmonics. for, ballasted in
psalm, hadn't the heart, once,

risen weightless, keyed to its own
dia-
tonic releases? couple to what, then, if not the
muffled reflections, dark mirrors of

that al-
together ob-
literated intent. wasn't this, in fact, what that
body proffered, no, not by the girth of its

shoulders nor the
pinch of its waist but
by the unsoundable depth of its hollows wherein, at
last, would find yourself fully refracted.

ON THE FUMIFEROUS NATURE OF LANGUAGE

. . . no, it's not fire, finally, that
goes to generate smoke, but smoke itself, in the
guise of
whisper, of so many soft, over-
lapping layers of loosened tresses, that

teases flame. brings it, in-
eluctable, to

focus. isn't it that, in
fact, that
draws, beguiles, takes you, each
time, under? what, retroflexive, renders the cells them-
selves
in-

candescent? yes, even here, in these
dark
dilapidated rooms, the
shutters shut and your own

long-standing lease
all-
but-expired, it's history itself, isn't it, you'd
fall through. the
body but pretext, the breath but

vector, would fuse as you went, catching as you
did on your own
smothered
combustibles. crouch to nothing, then, if not the

light you'd
lick, the long straws of
flame that, meticulously, you'd
suck, but only for the sake of some all

but im-
perceptible configuration.

GENESIS: A BELATED GAZE

. . . out of so many fleeting figures had
pos-
tulated solids, inter-
polated mass. pretended, hadn't we, that the

flesh would with-
stand its
wobbling reflections, the wrist its

loose
billowing shirtsleeves. we, who'd
taken possession, as we'd put it, of those de-
volving
properties, had claimed, as
went, perennity. why, then, such sudden
hesitations, we'd

ask, the
eye, that very
instant, slipping off the glazed flanks of
some sumptuous urn, its

begonias, by then,
gone fatuous. had the charm (what held us, once, as
if hallucinated, to the all-
too-
apparent) worn thin? its spell, in a spray of

prismatic particles, already
been broken? move, then, within the
with-

out. for there, where the
long corridors had gone, their walls dissolving in sheer
luminosity, might enter, at last, those
distant in-
timations.

wasn't that why they'd
grappled as they had, those wrestlers intent upon the
garlands, the braided laurels, of
loss? limbs locked in a

profusion of
unguents, wasn't it for that, that alone, that their
lips rounded to the

naught, that
word without words out of which, as
orifice, wind, light, and —effusive— those
long-
pronged shadows
had first erupted.

AN EXERCISE IN THE ORPHIC

. . . the mist, all morning, like
milky brushstrokes, lapped at the
low
golden boughs of the
oaks. were only here, you realized, for your own
ex-

travagation, the ribs but
rungs unto those
vi-

bratory expanses. would work yourself free, wouldn't
you, of all
this ornate signature, but only for the
sake of those weight-

less chords, vessels in which, on
pro-
clivity alone, might ride the tremor of
each
proffered octave. the body solvent, would enter, no,

not the woodlands beyond, but the
scherzo in
which laurel would
spring pulsatile out of each perfectly accorded air.

IN THE NAME OF THE NOUMENA

. . . had been lowered into this
querulous body but only for the sake of its
singular
releases. like

rooms, weren't they, those
sudden relegations, your breath as if
frescoed —but all
too fleetingly— in blue. blown hair, blown

heart, moving towards nothing
you'd
ever known, would kneel, wouldn't you, to the
noumena, receptacles, as you'd

called them, of the otherwise
ir-

retrievable. a world-without: wasn't that, indeed,
what you'd yearned for? what they, they
alone, like

reliquaries, retained? would wrap, wouldn't
you, about their least
life-
less particle. flesh, with your very lips, the very

syllables of so much
remote
ideation. bring, thus, to a tremor those ab-
sconded ex-
panses: what the breath, at last, might straddle and the

murmur, in
rending resuscitate.

TREMOLO

. . . here, even the smoke's
for
facetting, its every irresolute curl
struck sonorous. you who'd given yourself to those

scored dictations, had
squandered substance, hadn't you, but only for the
sake of

some remedial passage: for the drafts, as you'd
called them, wherein you'd enter, on

tonality alone, gardens awash in the
flora of an
al-
together forgotten in-

tent. what, though, could the tremolo recall that the
tongue couldn't? wedged earth,
it's

neither the dark breeze in all its delectation nor the
wild
ruffled foliage, but the wobbling of the
either in the

instantaneity of
all
origins.

ICON

. . . swelled to something far less than
any-
thing you'd ever known, than
language itself could

ever name.   vacua of the
in-

violate, about which, as if spectral,
earrings dangled less like
accessories than
twin

theurgical charms.

THEOPOLIS

. . . travelled on the back of those
worn
locatives, on whatever
sporadic vibrations they still e-

mitted. wasn't it towards that, that
illegible city, that
all language leaned? that you, caught in

such
tenuous currents,
journeyed? thinned, didn't you? thinned as
you entered those
pinched frequencies, o city that a

stylus scratched out of
waxed
tablets, then
left to the elements, in turn, to obliterate.

CREATION

. . . what if air itself
were little more than the air's
resonant chamber; the
wisteria, in all its knots and pendulosity, but the
vibratory surface of
some al-

together ob-
fuscated creation. you, cued to
nothing you'd
ever known, register, now, these

bars, measures, *contrappunti,* claiming them for your
very own when, in

fact, they're little more than the
random dictates of
what, in
passing, mistook your body for
instrument and your slightest breath for incantation.

VISTA

. . . little more than a glint, you'd
called it. than a
fugitive spark off the
face of some distant hillside to placate, on

occasion, the
grievous rib, that
all-
but irreparable fracture. blow

vocables, you'd
tell yourself. let breath alight upon those
abandoned reaches that
proffered, once,

relief. for here's but
angst. but re-
tention. but the chord withheld from its own
ac-

cording. isn't that why you'd wrap to the
deep pleats of
that chimeric gaze that, no, you
couldn't reclaim, but,

like some kind of luminous milk, duly assimilate.

WRITTEN IN WHITE: AN EXEGESIS

only written in white would the world, at last, become legible.

with words, that is, that hadn't yet undergone attribution, relegation, resolute fixity.

(as if enveloped, still, in the albumen of some initial intent).

pre-iconic, there in that suspended interval before the features, bit by bit, came to conflate.

came to alight, so doing, in discrete identities.

---

but a blush, at
first, of
luminous particles flooding the pores, a glow-
premonitory that no reflection could
catch nor zeitgeist
ap-
propriate.

---

for we always enter our own histories an instant after they've transpired.

are always, that is, an instant in default.

more like the memory of a garden that, for all its splendor, could neither be recalled nor entirely forgotten.

was why the tendons thrashed as they did.

why the bodies —arched convulsive like so much baroque statuary—attempted to break free from the fatality of such unremitting sequence.

seeking, as they did, a breach in the midst of that remorseless mechanism.

—a lapsus at the galactic heart of light—

. . . wasn't it that, just
that, that you'd fall through? for the
foam's
sake, wrap yourself in the

spume of so
many prearticulated particles, neither
yours nor

another's but the
wedged ebullience emerging out of such mutually
en-
acted annulments.

---

wherein, in those opaque mirrors, might awaken.

glean, from each other's released breath, the first unbidden syllables of that blanched alphabet.

PUBLISHER'S NOTE

The text of this *Collected* follows the text and layout of the first edition of each original volume collected within these covers. We have resisted the tempting notion of standardisation, choosing instead to reflect the original typesetting choices, given that the author's requirements were exacting – and even, in some cases, possibly unwise. Sobin wrote his poems longhand and then transcribed the texts on a typewriter. The latter gives the origin of his spacing and layout requirements, which caused some considerable discomfort to typesetters in the manual paste-up era, before the advent of computer-aided typesetting. Typewriter keys permitted a basic kind of textual positioning which subsequent word-processors, and then typesetting software, have long left behind – unless one uses a monospace font such as Courier. Using the full range of spacing and positioning options available in a page-design programme can *mostly* cure the problem however, and allow the author's somewhat painstaking requirements to be respected. An *exact* replica of the originals is not possible, however, because of differences in the footprints of the different fonts being used – and several different font- and leading-sizes were employed in the original books. I am confident however that the text here is as close as possible to the original versions brought together in the author's eight main collections.[1] This is why, for instance, the length of the space after a full stop (*period*) differs in various places here, why the gaps within lines vary somewhat across the span of the book – but not *within* a single collection – and why ellipses employ different lengths at different points in the book. The author mostly employed US spelling, and this has been respected here, but it should be noted that variations from this standard have also been respected; the occasional uses, therefore, of "grey", "travelling", "artefact", and "unravelled", to list but a few, reflect the author's own usage and are not the result of any intervention by the British publisher. A few minor typographical errors have been silently corrected.

I am indebted to Esther Sobin, her father's executor, and Andrew Joron and Andrew Zawacki, literary advisers to the author's Estate, for their

[1] Eagle-eyed readers who have access to the author's previously published books, might note – when making A/B comparisons – that the layouts in the 1995 selected poems, *By the Bias of Sound* (Talisman House), differ in places from the first published versions. We suspect that these differences do *not* indicate any rethinking on the author's part.

permission to republish this *Collected*, and, of course, to New Directions, who published the first editions of three of the books collected here – all are still in print – for their permission to reprint those volumes within these covers. I am further grateful to Ed Foster of Talisman House, publisher of the first edition of this book, who gave his blessing for this new edition.

Finally, I would especially like to thank the poet Martin Anderson, long a supporter of Sobin's work, and his correspondent over many years, for invaluable assistance with the copyediting of this edition.

Tony Frazer
August, 2025

www.ingramcontent.com/pod-product-compliance
Lightning Source LLC
Chambersburg PA
CBHW022101290426
44112CB00008B/508
* 9 7 8 1 8 4 8 6 1 9 9 4 4 *